THEO WILKERSON

THE
DIARIES
OF
PENCASSO

The Diaries of Pencasso
All Rights Reserved.
Copyright © 2020 Theo Wilkerson
v2.0

This is a work of fiction. The events and characters described herein are imaginary and are not intended to refer to specific places or living persons. The opinions expressed in this manuscript are solely the opinions of the author and do not represent the opinions or thoughts of the publisher. The author has represented and warranted full ownership and/or legal right to publish all the materials in this book.

This book may not be reproduced, transmitted, or stored in whole or in part by any means, including graphic, electronic, or mechanical without the express written consent of the publisher except in the case of brief quotations embodied in critical articles and reviews.

N'geniouz Minds LLC

ISBN: 978-0-578-23851-7

Cover by Theo Wilkerson. All rights reserved - used with permission.

PRINTED IN THE UNITED STATES OF AMERICA

Table of Contents

Phase I: The Relationship Diaries
1. Sick of Single (S.O.S.) 2
2. Struggles of Love 4
3. Thoughts of 5
4. Hopeless Love 6
5. Love Sick 8
6. Love Again 9
7. Love Experience 11
8. Vision of Love 12
9. Gypsy Queen 14
10. #2 B N Love 15
11. Basquiat Love 16
12. Happily ever After 17
13. Understanding 18
14. Strip 19
15. Communication 21
16. Loves Frustration 23
17. Date Night 24
18. Might be #BAE 25
19. Love Investment 26
20. That Type of Love 28
21. Dear Love 30
22. Love vindication 32
23. Masterpiece She 34
24. Her past 36
25. The Curious Case of Mr. Ex 38
26. Ex Chronicles Part 1 40
27. Reminded me 41
28. In Memory of 43
29. Fed Up 45
30. Black Lovebirds 47

31. Hidden Heartbreak 49
32. Confused by love 51
33. Fu*& Love 52
34. Suicide Love Letter 53

Phase II: The Sex Diaries
1. Pleasure Box 58
2. Untitled Sex 60
3. Shades of pink 62
4. Vivid Imagination 64
5. Wettification 66
6. Freaky Play 68
7. Nighttime temptations 70
8. Good Moaning 71
9. Another Nasty Jawn 72
10. Walls talk 73
11. Taste the Rainbow 74
12. Stress Reliver 76
13. Good Night/Good Morning 78
14. This Christmas 80
15. Tonight 82
16. Pleasure(Please her) 83
17. Submerged 84
18. Erotica 85
19. Good Dick 87
20. Regrets 88
21. Warning shot 90
22. OMG 92
23. Just Sex 93

Phase III: Life Writing Diaries
1. Letter to the King (Dedication to DaeQuan my Son) 98
2. Queendom (Message to Alliyah my daughter) 100
3. The Message 103

4. Meant to Heal (Mental Health) 105
5. Battles I 107
6. Battles II 108
7. Broken Mirror 109
8. Mass Eulogy 111
9. Who Shot ya 112
10. You Go Girl 113
11. Celibacy 114
12. Digital 115
13. Ms. Beautifully Complicated / The woman 117
14. Mr. Sidepiece 119
15. Glow Up 120
16. Without Women 121
17. Relationtrips 123
18. Don't love us 125
19. Destroy and Rebuild 127
20. New ambitions 129
21. Mind state 131
22. The System 133

Phase I:
The Relationship Diaries

Chapter I Introduction (The Relationships)

He was desperately searching for love, divorced and broken. A hopeless romantic born into a generation that didn't know of it. This thing called love, a feeling so quick to dismiss when dating, Instead of getting to know one another you find yourself cutting through the tape going in with a list of red flags. Before you even commence you're fighting with previous imprints. He was still practicing chivalry so he was a gentleman misplaced. He, he started to date maybe too soon as his heart was still injured. What he needed was therapist to heal him first, not a girlfriend, Yet he had a thirst to be loved.......

Sick of Single (S.O.S.)

I'm sick of being single
Nights is cold,
I, want a body to hold
I need her to help me build, her role GM
She forms the team
I don't want to do it alone
I'm like Fuck Love, If I'm not a part of
The hater in me
Living out my #relationshipgoals by liking other couples' digital imagery
Talking that #SINGLELIFE, I'm good with me
Drowning my moral code in Pornhub scrolls and Hennessey
Pretending she's moaning for me
All that for what?
What's the real reason, why I prefer to date me?
Is it that I have inability to compromise, or maybe because I been hurt before and now don't want to try
Maybe it's my expectations, they are just too damn high
If their no more good folks in this world then why is it that everybody single believes they're a good catch and can't find their compliment
The Irony Single, Believe, Compliment
This single shit gives me a complex
I'm trying to be a better man but, single got me only learning to be selfish
I'm so sick of single
Regardless of popular relief
It's overrated, I'm lost, alone spend way too much time with me
I sit back all day and listen to RnB tunes
Wake up in a romantic mood
Rollover, in search of getting one off

Only to find a body pillow
Missing my better half; searching, like where is she at?
I want to tell her a corny joke just to hear her laugh
Take her on trips to De Ja Vu, Barbados, Brazil the Cayman Islands too
My favorite curve is hers, Is her smile
I'm So sick of being single
I mean I'd rather walk in the park and hold hands, never go to bed mad
Wake up then make her breakfast
Have dinner surrounded by roses and candlelight
Propose and share with her my life
Scientist have proven in study that the love of a woman expands the life
I want to do right, take a leap of faith and sacrifice
This #SingleAF is overrated, I'm good, To busy loving me
So, I say in hopes that the Gram will believe, On the contrary
I'm a walking contradiction this single life is a sickness for me

I'm a hopeless romantic searching for my peace……I never said it would be easy So as I embark on this journey in search of I have to be willing to deal with the Struggles of Love

Struggles of Love

Do we fall in love with the feeling?
Or just the theory of
When it's not perfect, do we remember the reason for?
Why he/she was so perfect before
What happened to the compatible flow?
See love is made in moments
When the opportunity is there
Are we willing to fight for it?
It's not always easy
I need you to want and not need me
Let's stop the comparisons of past failures
Me to him and She to you
Instead let's take those failed versions of heart and write a new one
Lessons in love
Dispense our efforts in one another's happiness
Never leave home without that I love you kiss
Make that phrase "go to sleep mad" not exist in this relationship
Let's talk it out now, agree to disagree
Then fuck it out
Rebuild the trust, A couple must continue to date
Those pet names and roles still exist of Zaddy and BAE
Let's go back to what we originally thought love was
Take the time to learn and love that one
These are just some of my Struggles with Love

In my own head, At times playing Russian roulette with a fully loaded chamber, she loves me, she loves me not cheating as to avoid the danger leads to what are believed to be Thoughts of .

Thoughts of…

Thoughts of a hopeless romantic
I really need this to work
Tired of the six-month trials just to make It past the flirt
I can't get this time back, now that's time wasted
With pretty faces that just end up as failed situations
Then we move on with baggage, sometimes closure is the curse
Trying to give her a fresh slate but, bring forth the hurt
Yet, I'm constantly giving relationship advice and seeing my ideologies work
Which has me wondering about my own damn worth
Like what about me why can't I find her?
Wanting so bad to operate like the golden loves of the past
Longing to be a husband and not settle for baby dad
Liking social media features about what love looks like
Yet tormented by the emptiness in my own life
My optimism, is the next one is Mrs. Right and not Ms. Right now
Each one is a bit different; not like the past
Her skin is light while her melanin a bit darker
She's thin while the others a walking traffic stopper
I find myself constantly failing at love and I just don't get enough
Love, to me I guess is like learning how to walk
You fall and get back up
Simply try, and try again
The thoughts of a hopeless romantic

The once hopeless lover is slowly becoming heartless due to his environment….A scorned gentleman after slowly giving in and giving unto her. She made him feel Hopeless

Hopeless Love

Born into a generation that doesn't know love
We all just want to fuck
Meanwhile, my hopeless ass out wondering is there anyone out there still making love?
Building up that foundation of trust or is it just that phase of lust ?
The prequel to another bad break up
I just want to find true love, like what's that experience
I'm tired of throwing dollars up to her for temporary compliments
She's diluting my vision playing the role of an illusional love interest
Now I'm blaming her and It's not her fault at all she's just good at her job
A broken romantic searching for love with Badoo apps, POF and Tinder swiping right hoping for a connect and text
Back of my mind hoping that the first meeting is not a catfish
#relationshipgoals
Well what the fuck are those, how can I replicate what I never seen?
The game of love is something told not sold, taught and learned and I
Well I've never been exposed
My role models were developed from Love and hip-hop episodes
See generationally, we believe in the toxicity
That he/she hate me delivery
The emotional instability, lack of creativity and absence of chivalry got us suffering
Burying it in the physical moments but, what happens when that's lost
When her body doesn't look twenty something no more and my dick requires that blue assistance to get up
Will we then find love?
Or remain lost in between hashtags and all the good ones are gone debate

Can we conversate and build something real
Catch chills just from his/her appeal
Or remain hopelessly searching for love
When we think it's an easy button
We lack putting forth the effort, mind corrupting the heart with thoughts of we shouldn't have to work hard
We are the Hopeless

Continued missing at love due to my own selfless abilities to discipline myself, find help at healing, defining relationship goals. The once hopeless romantic had now fell ill. He was now Love Sick

Love Sick

Hopeless romantic
Stranded on love street
Thirsty, like why does this feeling keep avoiding me
I was told nice guys finish last and to that phrase I didn't listen
As a gentleman it is part of my algorithm
Maybe it's the system, or the woman that I'm picking or maybe
My impartial position on fuck boy living because I seem to come in her life after that
My vision is to build a life with her and the kids, send them to the grandparents and take her on a Baecation
Destination is her choice,
I only ask that we turn the phones off
The intention is to get lost in us
My heart's desire is to be cured from this love sickness besides,
What's Love anyway?
Not by definition but, can it exist in spirits
If so, what am lacking to be placed in that position
Where love songs begin to remind me of you, and in pictures my smile is radiant because it's taken next to you
I'm lovesick
A hopeless romantic searching for a cure to the hurt

Distracted and mesmerized by such a tantalizing figure as she
We embarked on a journey in search of magical moments to fill with Love again

Love Again

Wondering what I'm missing to be in the position to love again
Fighting through feelings
The heart of a lonely man
Imprisoned within my own emotions
I got trust issues
Feeling indebted to her yet, spend my time thinking about you
Confused, about the complicated situation
I, got commitment issues
Find myself looking for a reason to run and
It doesn't take much
Already fragile, cracked and broken
The minute I start seeing ex-girl visions
That's reason for relationship intermission
I need a minute
During the down time I suggest you see other niggas
I'll carry my baggage to some other woman
Coincidentally, I'm no better than her
Still giving her power cause She had me thinking
Through assumptions that I ain't shit
Her lips never formed those words but, that's what I read from it
So on to the next now lacking the confidence I started with
First mistake was believing it, Ego shattered, I was a mess
My gentleman behavior sided for ratchetness
When I should've been healing
Instead I was hurting feelings dealing with the past BS
Trying to hide my emotions in moments of sex
Had to forgive myself, fight the man in the mirror for clearer vision
Ask God, to cleanse my spirit
Then wait patiently for her to assist me in my journey and
Show me
How to love again

Through the eyes of an injured heart, he sees this emotion as distorted. He was lacking the positive experience to believe in monogamy. Never believing he to be her only one. She did not belong to him it was only his turn for a love experience

Love Experience

I want to become the slave to her rhythm
The boom bap to her hip hop
The ending high note to her opera
I want to be the subject in her notebook for lonely hearts
I want her to embed me so deep in her thoughts that
I become her daydream
Be the subject of her photography
I want to cover pages and pages of her diary
With her speaking of how I am her king
I want her to save text messages from me, just to go back and read
I want to be her man crush
Have her stay in lust while still experiencing the art of falling in love
I want to make our two hearts become one
Become lost in her presence
Her essence is the symbology of a cherry moon under diamond stars
She is to me what I am to her
A love experience

After experiencing love for the first time in what seemed like forever, he had a Jones for her. She was his substance abuse, his healing. He needed her to go on or so he thought, any other muse would become a tragedy, his vision was skewed he loved her.

Vision of Love

Caught up in her rapture
She got me questioning my own swagger
Mirage vision, all I see in her eyes is ever after
I mean the hue is different
Conversations with her got me seeing the full kaleidoscope
Whereas, before it was only colors of blue
A representation for hope
I hear every music note, violin string and piano key
I no longer hear as a consumer but, with the same quality ears of a hit producer
Together we are engineering beautiful music
She's the lead on vocalist on the album titled "a movement toward the future"
The video for the single filmed everything
Rain, bended knee I present her with a ring
Ask her the ultimate question
Will you please bare my last name?
Become my happily ever after
Be there to coach me through the pain
Develop what I don't see and mold me into a better man
Replace my sadness with moments of laughter
I don't want to awaken another day and you not be lying next to me
For you I want to inhale faithfulness, and exhale loyalty
Please be my 21 percent of Oxygen
I need you to breathe
I love you!
You are the perfect mixture of that love potion number 9 elixir
Your kisses are my unlimited prescription
She is both my detox and my addiction
This loves so much deeper than physical appearance
I'm in I love with her spirit

She is my apple and I her Adam
The other side to my half heart and her half makes me whole
I am her body, she is my soul
With her I want to grow old
She is my vison of love

Now since meeting her, He now has tunnel vision all he sees with her, she is one part Lisa Bonet, one part Erykah Badu. Crazy, Sexy Cool she was what some would call a witch not evil he called her his Gypsy Queen....

Gypsy Queen

I want to write for you
Craft you a feature
Original piece, I tore it up wasn't good enough it had to be much deeper
To invigorate your intellectual mind
Mathematically inclined in her study of numerology
So, if 9 – 3 = 6 which bring about terms of harmonious and the square root of 9 is 3
We are seemingly a perfect fit
Her energy is like a talk show where Erykah Badu is the host
Lisa Bonet and Lauryn Hill the guest and they discuss realms of metaphysics and their individual spirits
She must be a descendent of both Oshun and Aprodite
Her eyes lure you in
I awaken with visions of her with crystal balls and head wraps as a hypnotist
I'm under her spell
Their closed minds speculate witchcraft when she is complex simplicity
Walking artwork yet so much more than vivid imagery, there are many layers to she
Each one part of her individuality or as she would say different moons and astrology's
Conversations intriguing in each one she teaches
She is that gypsy queen

With a woman such as she, so much quality substance, so much integrity and discipline. How could a single man resist her. It was almost forced upon him 2 B N Love……..

#2 B N Love

Its thoughts of her that allow me to dream in 3D and in color
My vivid imagination has me seeing
Her fully clothed yet I see her naked
Mouth salivating, tempted to taste it
The anticipation's got me like
I literally want to fall in love with her
Be pussy whipped, need her kiss to get through the day
Feel like something is missing until she says BAE, I'm on the way
I want her to become my priority
Send her random messages throughout the day
It's with her I can find the proper use of emojis and hashtags texting
I want to be loyal to her show her my growth
How I've long since left playboy alone
I want to put down my phone, no secret code
Check if you want
See I'm too busy cheating on my girl using her alter ego
I just want to be in love
I want to fall in love again be the center of her attention
Become the picture she's posting consistently as her #MCM
I just want to Be In Love, slip and fall all the way in

It wasn't enough to just be in love, I wanted to stand up in it, be committed wholeheartedly something I'd never experienced prior to meeting her. I wanted to paint love as a masterpiece and sculpt us. I guess what I was looking for was her to be my Basquiat…..

Basquiat Love

This is that middle of night how does it feel love
That I was just thinking about you and wondering how ya day was
That nan nan ni boo boo I beat you home love
Teasing you but you got a warm bath, dinner and foot rubs type love
That roses just because it's Wednesday and you're my forever woman crush
That loyalty love, dedicated in you I trust
Tore me down over time just to build me up
Hand crafted to portray the man you want
I am yours
I Rise N grind, work hard to spoil us
I see poetry in motion every time she walks
Fall deeper in love every time she talks
Started out in lust, then fell in love with her
Now I struggle to stand up
The definition of work, a hand-crafted sculpture of us
We live that Basquiat Love
Loves masterpiece, it was she that became my thesis
Which is why I got my Graduate degree
She compliments every word I speak,
Her name is my favorite word in the vocabulary
Together we are the perfect chemistry
Our hands molding one another to become the perfect us
This is a love founded by Basquiat

With the creation of us, a love everlasting or so I thought, she was all I could see in a room full of beautiful people. I do! I wanted her to be my Happily ever after

Happily ever After

The first chapter of happily ever after
Often days spent video chatting and laughter
Both of us the co-authors of distant lovers
She pens the even pages; I have the responsibility for the odd offers
Exploring possibilities of forever with hearts protected
He can't fail at love again and she only has one feeling left
Two broken hearts seeking to mend with togetherness
The journey epic and intense to bury each other in a rabbit hole of sorts
Thoughts of a hopeless romantic
Who could've thought that after a decade plus two
They'd still have conversation points and mutual interest
Stemming from those thoughts of what should but, never was
The energy is great, the two have a lover's chemistry
Sacrificing their fears of for probability
Planting seeds with a foundation that stems from loyalty
She is the calmness to his insanity
While he plays her complimentary
The reason he believes the two have a want and a need
Pictorial memories painted of beach front views, cruise liners and exotic cuisine
Passport stamps, Lips connected in kiss under moons in foreign places
Holding hands while engaging in wine tasting
Body craving, creating a sexual stimulation with
The ultimate goal is to replace the word "like" with another four-letter word that has a deeper meaning "love" in the climax chapters
The book we write together is titled "Happily ever after"

Finally feeling secure during the healing process, he reflects on how they got here
A relationship is simple as long as you go into open minded with belief and using communication to succeed the two find Understanding…..

Understanding

He gives her good dick and understanding
Tie it all together that's the definition of what a man is
He'll support her dreams and ambitions while placing her body in deep penetrating positions
He Keeps her well-fed, promoting her bedroom behavior
Be his freak, be nasty
He damn near dares you
He fills her head up with a complimenting dialect that makes her feel like her Government name is Beautiful, Gorgeous and Elegant
He intellectually stimulates when he simply posing the question "Bae, How was her day?"
Unlike some, He shows through his actions that she's the chosen one defining relationship status with loyalty and providing that life of emotional luxury;
His intent is his woman doesn't want for anything
Which in turn keeps the doors closed to the sidepiece
He fulfills her needs, peaks her interest, and with his tongue
He not only explores intimate places but, puts together sentences and speeches during
conversation
He gives her full understanding

This understanding doesn't happen without both parties learning to love one another naked. Learning the emptiness, the flaws seeing each one for who they are. An argument ensues off a bad day So I ask her to remember when we met I asked you to Strip for me....

Strip

What I want you to do right now; Is Strip for me
Lye right here on this bed in the nude
Take off your clothes and give me what I want
Strip for me
I get that you barely know me,
Girl he got some got some audacity but, before you curve me
The Strip for me terminology wasn't meant in the physical sense
See when I said STRIP, I meant STRIP yourself of that hate and discontent
You hold towards me because of what he did or even the one that went before him
Or her because you were experimenting, and in your feelings said you were done with men!
So, I ask you to strip for me
Allow me to learn you and love you like only I know how to do
In return I'm willing to strip too butt naked exposing my pride and ego to you.
Become a student of you and allow you to teach me how to love
Because I am by no means perfect neither is any man walking but, what I am is a man with perfect flaws
Placed there by the hands of God to be molded by a woman
However, you won't let these moments exist because your past insist that I ain't shit
You say all I do is work and provide and you still feel lonely as I'm not in touch with your emotional side
Let me remind you that's just how I was raised
See poppa was a rolling stone, we knew it was payday cuz pops wasn't coming home
My mother never had that support so all I know is grind
I can work the hell out of a 9 to 5 even put in that overtime
To give you everything you desire

See baby I promise it's only you
I'd work till I'm exhausted to give you any planets you choose to include the Moon
Just make a wish, I'll be your genie and with me you're not limited to 3
But, before any of this can happen, I need you to Strip for me. Allow the possibility.

For me to know you better and have any chances of WE I simply had to use the lost art of communication

Communication

I simply want to know how your day went
Entrance
Me on bended knee, rose in between lips
In preparation to taste it
Communication
Let's discuss religious theories and politics or why Tariq still being bad shit
Let's talk about everything and nothing
I don't care that you acting different, I want to know why?
Where do I fit in, what can I do to take what's broken at the moment and get it fixed
See that's how we become best friends and for me that's important
See first time around she wasn't, felt she was too sensitive so I stop talking
Couldn't deal with the emotions
Communication is key
There's a difference between intimacy and fucking
We can lay up doing nothing outside of talking and booty rubbing
I mean act like it's that time of the month and it wasn't
See I found that's what makes it last and creates those forever moments
See, I know her body so well Just from the talking
I tell her wait just as she is about to start cumming
Hold it for me, wait on me a moment
Switch to her favorite position and continue stroking
Its communication that plays the critical role in relationship goals
That's the secret that allows you the ability to grow old
Make love to the intellect cause at some point the physical goes
In doing so, you know your best friend inside and out
Think about the kids a generation that seemingly don't know we at least had 90s RnB you hear what's played on the radio

The communication at home would stimulate that role model shit
Now she don't give a fuck about a hot girl summer and he won't fall for thirst trapping pics
Communication is how
When we having them fuck you days , we kiss, make up and go on
That I'm going to get something to eat, shit you hungry
Sublime I'm sorry, see without the communication you can't see the apology in this
Because we don't take the time to learn our partners love language
These are words I jotted on napkin while attending a silver anniversary dinner
Inspired by endless love, feel like I learned late and want to pass it on
Learning and Teaching
Communication

Though the communication and understanding is good he still finds himself suffering from the evils of. At times Loves comes with frustration……

Loves Frustration

So, frustrated with love
He can't see the one right in front of him
Rather chase miss lady that's constantly curving him
Than, the one trying to share words with him
Finding it hard to trust my heart again as
It keeps misleading my feelings
Now, in the midst of healing I'm over thinking situations
Lacking the patience, so no relationship of his seems to make it past the lust stages
He finds a way to separate from her temptation
He keeps using the same verbiage
"I'm Self-destructive, baby it's not you, it's me I don't deserve ya"
Dating in bias, shallow see he's blinded by curves first
The pole dancing vegan versus Miss Lady of distinction
The one with one or two kids, workout and seeking a college degree
Lies to himself not to get involved "She doesn't have time for me"
Though she's probably better for me giving substance and guidance
She looks better with me twerking I'd probably cheat regardless and she's the perfect side chic
Though she brings less to the table, I'd rather break bread with her
Funny, how tales from your Ex can have emotional control over the current ones
The heart was broken once, now he is
Frustrated with this thing called love.....

Old head told me once that the key to relationships son is
to continue to date so me and the lady ageed on that advice
sometimes she'd pick, sometimes it was on me but, we always kept
a Date Night....

Date Night...

Before Dinner
You're supposed to set the table
That's exactly what she did
Oh, tonight she's in her bag
Sun dress on with them heels
Forcing me to stare
She is the most beautiful distraction
Candy lady walk, looking like her precipitation tastes like grape now and laters dipped in Mango juice when she orgasmically erupts
Apologies ma'am for the mannish thoughts
I should be on my best gentleman behavior but, I do admire your walk off
I'm saying you entered in the building and gave the atmosphere life
No words needed to be said, they eye's say Jesus Christ!!
A never before seen image, she was a walking paradise
Now conversation over meals exposing her intellect, but the cut of that dress exposes her breast
The perfect combination for seduction
She senses it using her woman's intuition, like boy what you looking at?
Distracted by mannish thoughts, I can't wait till dinner is over
Four leaf clover in my pocket hoping I get lucky enough to touch her where I'm focused
We take walks in park, at that point I present her with roses
She smiles, exposing her best curve as we discuss the next episode of nightly events
Then gently apply that kiss that leads to multiple orgasms
Before Dinner you're supposed to set the table
After the meal I'll do the dishes

After a few dates and my heart going back and forth with the mind. I realized for the first time in a long time that I just might be qualified. I just might be BAE....

Might be #BAE

He might just be BAE
He cooks, clean and compliments me domestically
Speaks to me only in confidence using compliments
Like damn boo you getting thick
Though we don't always agree yet never disrespects me
He might just be BAE
Takes time to get to know me, forcing the orgasmic release effortlessly
Bae can indulge in me mentally, stimulating only positive energy
He is my therapy, in him I can release my uncertainty
He bags up those insecurities, they become building opportunities #hegotme
Bae works with me, balances my emotional reactions with his logical thinking
Displays loyalty to me constantly working to chip away at my protective walls and expose my deepest feelings #Baehealsme
A Visionary, reading in between hidden lines
Without words he's tries when I don't see his efforts, in my feelings and don't want to be bothered
#BAEcomfortsme
Using Good dick and conversation, I reach that pleasure principle
Bae strengthens me when I feel weak
Given the opportunity, BAE might just be me!!

Though he is fighting with potential heartbreak, the back and forth of commitment turned argument. He still longs for those moments and is willing to bet it all on as he realizes he can't make it without Love's Investment.....

Love Investment

We both came to the table all in
Suitcase full of emotions and feelings
Both secretly in search of progressive healing
A clean slate
Fuck him, Fuck her
See we gotta move on
What's behind door number one
Is it the same old love song
Melancholy plots of mistrust
Fall in love too fast and can't stand up
Legs broken from past relation trips
I never truly healed from her
And you are heartbroken for him
Still we decide the time is right to go through the emotions of
Possibility, like two broken hearts can become one
The injured reserve are we
But a great trainer can form us
So, we call all in
Bet on the half ass hand as the dealer has laid a straight set
It is not a royal flush guarantee
In the future we could break up
End up as another love lost
But, I'm tired of failure
I want to be with her
Enamored by her thought
Let's talk, figure it out
Past failures have brought about doubt that I can make you happy
Like I'm lost, no clue what intimacy is without the physicality
I was not enough to love those before you
What makes this a different outcome
When 1+1 is two no matter what language we speak

He hurt you badly
Cheated, had you feeling as if you were not good enough
Caught him in the act he said that she was meaningless
Just a situational nut
Baby our floor was wet from separated communication and I
Slipped and fell inside her walls as support trying to hold us up
With a second and third chance he'd do better
They say a man got a big ego but, a woman's injured pride is through trust
So, I brought a seamstress with me
Trying to take measurements, craft the perfect fit
I'll be honest I'm scared to death
My life savings combined with yours sacrificed for US to be the best
Testing the market that's often up and down
But, without investment we can't be rich

After investing terms of endearment with hopes to become best friend material, he wrote a letter to manifest to the universe, let her into his darkness and release his demons. Dear Love......

That Type of Love

I want to dance with you, to the lyrics of our own musical
Have you co-write and produce the next chapter of us
A romance novel based on our Love, Trust, Understanding and Loyalty
Develop a love like I fell in it and couldn't get up
I want to look at you and ask who sent you and where did you come from?
The type of love like every anniversary I want to send your mother and father thank you cards
At least 50 of them
Speak to you in a poetic language using haikus, metaphors and similes
That type of love that got me thanking God daily then smile because you wake up next to me
I want that love that take trips overseas to places where we will rarely be scene
No phones baecations, the world doesn't exist it's just you and me
In the creation of epic monologues and refreshing memories
I mean I want that type of love they sung about in the 70s
Where she's my living , breathing love song
That 90's RnB
Jodeci, I can't leave you alone I'm "feenin" for her daily
Tunnel vision blinding me to anything except her views
I'm talking the type of love that has me so into you that from a distance too far
I'm overcome by that Babyface and Toni Braxton feeling as though I need you to breathe
I want to grow with you, develop a partnership where
You are my rib, and I am your lung
I need you to breathe
I want to experience Love

In search of and hoping this was right. He settled in, locked and focused on developing something not before dealt with. Dear Love……

Dear Love

A hopeless romantic desperately in search of love from her
Hoping that she will quench my thirst
A snack nah
I'm tired and hungry
From her I want an appetizer, entrée and dessert
I write for her in verse like to whom it may concern
Dear love I desire
Where are thou?
Over time I've grown from caterpillar to butterfly
Removed my shallow shell
I am now ready to don the crown
Receive the blessing of you and be removed from this lonely hell
To stop eating rotten apples and indulge in passion fruit
I know now due to growth that
I had to go through what I went through
In preparation for you
The evils of cheating to conceal heartbreak was needed
When I was innocent, she didn't believe it
So, I made it a reality
Apologies became the compromise
I no longer could see forever in her eyes
The deepness was gone, only saw maybes and tomorrow
Broken communication lines
Shutting down instead of talking it out
Thinking I was protecting her feelings really, selfishly protecting mine
Ego shattered as each and every window is broken out
Wondering to myself what is real love about?
I've only been content in relationships, how do I reach that thing called happiness

I hope this letter reaches you and you answer my terms of endearment
Please know I am still healing but, need you to complete the process
Close the loop, make me whole again
Dear Love

Believing he was freeing himself of his past. He went in 10 toes down giving her the crown and throne of his heart. She became his Jones and in her instead of himself he sought out happiness and Love's Vindication....

Love vindication

I'm finally ready to experience love like I know I can
Seeking a reason in her
I'm in love with the process of making love
A natural phenomenon
But, at some point I want to fall in it
Live past the infatuated premise in the beginning, plant a seed of loyalty and ask
Do you know we're in it?
Comfortably age together, write chapters of a love novel as co-authors
I want her to be my sponsor
Become coconspirators to the scripture of love
Real talk, I don't even know if real love is a thing at all, but I want to experience it
I mean I don't know if it's simply a term, maybe it's a figment of my imagination
Maybe the thought torments my own sanity borderline questioning my rationale
I want to feel that chemistry when making love to her
Know the proper angle, stroke and next move when submerged in her waterworks
She feels like heaven on earth and I
Speak to her in a poetic language haikus and similes that finish her sentences
I am in search of freedom to love without cause
They define this as unconditional like, I want to be the guy that
When asked why you love all her?
My response is why would I not
Translation she has me lost, I'm clueless and the reason is not pinpointed
Meaning I have no control of my heart it's hers

I want to solidify loves existence
Heart, Soul, body and mind tied together
She is my addiction, my hearts stimulation
In this gorgeous Queen I see love's vindication.

Feeling overjoyed and exuberant. High off love she a Basquit designed for his heart. Her outlines perfect she was the Masterpiece…..

Masterpiece She

A Struggling artist
Inspired by her vision
Trying to recreate the perfect picture
Only using word variations, metaphors and similes
However, her movements are in rhythm,
Her steps sounding like a 90's RnB love song
She is an alluring vision, A masterpiece
Painted by hand
Her canvas silk sheets and angel wings
The centerpiece for every room she enters
Bow down, bended knee to pay homage all hail the Queen!
So, I asked a brilliant artist, how do you craft perfection?
The response, it must first start with her smile, that's her most perfect curve
Her happiness will be her signature
Line after line of this creates the perfect verse
A melodic lullaby, "Beautiful possibilities"
Apply a variety of colors as she is a fascinating image, eye-catching
Compose her using intellect in your verses
You must make love to her mind, relieve her heart from the hurt
Don't promise her you're different, but show her
Caress her imperfections and help her heal
Display to her your loyalty and desire to build
Become her flawed perfection and it seems
Since briefly meeting her my pen has been busy futility attempting to synchronize words of her beautiful imagery
She is a photographer's dream model, no matter the angle she'll make it easy
The cover girl for any magazine, such a blessing it is to have her in your design

She is crafted perfectly, I thank God daily and pray that she is 100% for me
As this woman is my complete masterpiece.

We all have baggage, none lighter than the rest at entrance. It is our responsibility to decipher and sort it out during the journey. The unfortunate selection of our previous was needed in preparation for another. Its a thing we attempt to let go and forget. Her past……

Her past

She must have a fuckboy syndrome
Be a magnet to the bullshit
This is like every man that she chooses to deal with
Problem is see she likes a project
So, fed up with her own choices that she no longer sees the realness
When she does, automatically assume him to be fraud
Interview with a vampire
Text messages read
Show me the man, delete the boy
She's forced to build up these walls
Then there's me
I just want to fall
So Deeply in love, that I drown in her existence
Yet her past makes it hard to deal with
Got me locked out, knocking on deadbolted doors with no one home like let me talk to you for a minute
Maybe I can be of assistance and give balance to your circadian rhythm
I want to mend your fractured heart; help you heal quick
Here's my ears for your struggle, allow me to be your therapist
See I can relate, I too have made some past mistakes
Had some growth issues
I mean as I pen this
I'm questioning does loyalty really exist?
Is monogamy a real thing?
Or is my imagination playing tricks?
Yet in still I want to be in a knelt position
Box half open with some bling
Followed by the words
Would you please do me the honor and marry me?
I want to fight through the hard questions

In search of a life partner
Contrary to popular belief these single nights are way darker
Miss lady fuck boys are not your only option
I am opportunity knocking

I couldn't get through to her, she was so stuck with trust issues, Though I attempt to fight through it for her. The realization was that our past still had power and we had yet to heal from these separately. Maybe we moved too fast and were still suffering from a Case of Mr. Ex……

The Curious Case of Mr. Ex…

I'm not him
Mr. verbal abuser, but you still love him tho
He just talks to you crazy cuz with showing affection he struggles too
Mr. Girl I know I shouldn't, yet you still return his text,
Secretly in your phone Mr. Good Dick, you ain't got over him yet
Allow yourself to be strung along characters for sex, yet he fucks you when you ain't wet
That's the play, 57 fake out
See you pursued thinking you need closure
However, very aware of why the relationship ended
Stressed you out, thinking you're not enough as he's DMing hidden women
I play faithful and I get
I awaited this opportunity for a minute
He fucked up, I slid in
With him the dick is hung different but, without consistent orgasm
If the pipe isn't enough to please you with me, you get steady tongue
You will cum!
I am your security blanket, Mr. Fix it
Not afraid of your broken heart I'll assist in mending
I told the truth from jump but, due to Ex man past behaviors you have problems believing.
Your time he stole and with me, it's those intimate moments that are valuable
I know what you thinking this is more than just a beginning
I'm trying to go the distance, lifelong with my last name on the ending of misses
Let him go, give me a minute you'll forget he exist
The only sad face from those following
You can't move on by allowing him to play coy

Get a man, leave the boy
Stop blocking me due to the case of your Ex…Move on

She tries, just not ready yet. I can't keep it together as now she has triggered my PTSD and anxiety in relationships, we cordially decide to relive Ex Chronicles cause unhealed we have given them power…….

Ex Chronicles Part 1

I told her
Speak to me in the language of love
Let's not discuss your heartbreak, but what led up to his mistake
Let's converse about what it takes to replace that ache
Hello love, goodbye heartbreak
I want to commit to you, build a foundation of trust and faith
Old heads told me young man it's a thin line between love and hate
Let's place that in the center and play tug of war with give and take
I'm willing to compromise
Grown ass man, no more shallow eyes my favorite curve on you
Ms Lady is your smile
I want to ingest your happiness and create an atmosphere of smiles and laughter
You continue in your role of Queen
I'll be the King and Jester
Multi-tasking; while asking all the right questions
I want to learn to love you better, our theme music Chrisette Michelle "A couple of forever's"
They say one man's trash is another man treasure and that two broken hearts can become whole together
Fuck past transgressions, let's move on toward progression
I plan to be in love with you like it's my profession and I don't want to get fired
I don't nothing half ass, Capricorn traits, I'm all the way in
Signed your homie, lover and best friend anxiously awaiting our next conversation
Let's build together and put that work in to create A Love that'll last
I AM NOT HIM!

The constant back and forth of two personalities broken led to her during argument reminding me....

Reminded me

She reminded me
That lately I've been acting different
Seems like every Friday night you out investing in strippers
I really didn't care much, cause you did that when I met you
Told me don't let it shatter your confidence BAE
I only got eyes for you
However, now I'm confused see yours words were found to be irrelevant
You out there in the streets with criminal intent
You got an interest arising from the late night twerking and tits
See there's one in particular
You know her
The popular, light skin thick sister
I Kind of want to call her a bitch
But out of respect for sistahood, I'll digress
With her word is so much of your money is spent
Those distracting actions led me to do some research and I found out you got a whole baby with this chick
Thought I was special, and we had a love investment
See this only proves you're not the man I thought you were but a coward because
It was not from your mouth that I found out, no wonder you don't want to get me pregnant
Your families at another house
I'm fed up, thought I could trust you and with you knew what love was about
But since I can't pack your shit and get the fuck out
Just promise me one thing, you'll be a better father to him, then you were man to me
You'll protect his heart with yours
The opposite of what you did to me

You won't lie to him because if finds the truths in the lies they'll only hurt more
Let him know that he's your son and for him you live for
I'm hurt and with love can't deal anymore
Worst part is I'll leave you and take it out on him
Cause we bounce in and out of relationships without unpacking baggage first
I want to hug you now but, it'll hurt too much
I want to give you a good-bye kiss, but it'll lead me in prison
So, I'll leave you with this
You are forgiven you good for nothing nigga

Baggage! she was right I really should've told her about the mistake I made with miss thang and funny me and her ain't even close to a possibility she was simply a fling now my love has become simply the Memory of....

In Memory of

I'm so sick of this loneliness
Laying here alone in this bed, grown ass man squeezing pillows
Incomplete feeling of royalty as I lack a queen
My mind transcribes why to my heart as I'm twisted up in knots
In memory of that thing called love
See this ain't that miss my ex boo type of poem because what I truly miss is the experience, they call love
Like I want to enjoy date night, conversations over candlelight
Her laying securely over my chest expressing how her co-workers is testing her nerves
That love experience that comes from her prepping a meal and you look at your boo body like Lord Thank you
She is unreal, She got that kill em in flats, kill em in heels
Pilates curves that work both that sundress and them sweats and lets not talk about yoga pants
That right there damn
I miss the experience of frivolous fights and I know now that they test both patience and foundation
I miss the experience of make-up sex
That recovery stimulation is the greatest and reminds you that the bond is strong
I want to hear love songs again and Its like she's in the lyrics
I want that can't wait to clock out, get home to her smile as it fulfills my spirit
I'm sick of acting like being single is the shit, fuck a body count
I want fulfillment someone I can share and build with
Love goes in stages and sometimes it ain't easy but, well worth the experiences
For her I want to be her perfect complement and from her I want to be wanted and not needed
Fuck these drunken nights and lonely thoughts

I pen these words from the balcony with Hennessey filled cups, missing her
In memory of this thing called love

Realizing that it wasn't enough the pain, the baggage, the inability left to trust decided to leave the situation. In attempt to fully heal, The both of us were Fed up…..

Fed Up

I'm so fed up with love
I'm hating on my favorite movie roles fuck Darrius Lovehall
Then there's love and basketball fuck Quincy McCall and Monica Wright
Playing for the next score
I'll remedy that don't pick me and I'm taking my ball
No one plays
Love is a dangerous game, got my heart in it
4th and 1 line of scrimmage and got injured
Ball game
Gave my heart to the wrong one
Left with these hurt feelings
Staring at these pictures of her and then another nigga
She told me I was too soft
I didn't dress the part and couldn't protect her image
Or reminded me how I'm a pushover and let her have her way all the time
Yet in my mind I was doing this thing called compromise
She said I wasn't equipped with enough dick and I left her unsatisfied
She singlehandedly destroyed my pride
Any chance of me moving on left with her
Now I use the cliché when discussing my flaws
I simply love too hard that's all
Loved her more than I loved myself and in essence I became lost
Questioning the death of monogamy
See loyalty is overrated, get you a side piece
Now I only trust what I can see
She told me I wasn't good enough and I never unpacked that baggage I bought
Find myself trying to love through the hurt

So, scared to fail at it that ultimately, we never pen the first verse
Left again lonely maybe I deserve the heartbreak
This heartache of a broken heart is a pain I can't shake
I'm really a good man in disguise that doesn't want to hurt her, so I leave when times seem to hard
Signed a man broken with a lonely heart

Just as he thought it was over his heart found refuge again. Thinking they were meant to be maybe they were simply Black Lovebirds....

Black Lovebirds

She's too busy blocking the feelings to progress
He's too vulnerable to enjoy the process
Feeling as though trusting his heart is a forgotten concept
While she carries the neglect from a previous ex and takes it out on all men
Where does that leave him?
So, the question is can they let love in?
At least come to a mutual agreement to simply try
See, he's fascinated with her ambitions, feeling her vibe
Going in with the kindest intentions to protect her feelings and mend her broken heart
Though he is only man and will make mistakes
Hoping to be coached through and not have a sealed fate
With him, she feels protected by his presence and hears loyalty in the words recited
Successful on her own, will she allow him to buy in? or simply pretend till she's bored
They have a connection, that kinetic energy it takes to create a love everlasting
I'm talking that since the day we met speech, celebrating a silver anniversary
Yet they seem to sabotage the greatness with hatred from their past and no role models of what a healthy relationship is
He is controlled by her, she by him so instead of falling in
Their puppets that fight love with sword and shield
So, when their paths crossed, they lost the moment due to fear
Him refusing to show his emotional side
She can't bear to be hurt again
So, they're left wondering what if?
Black Lovebirds

Maybe I'm a serial dater, Cause at relationships I continue failing. What am I in search of? The possibility of love, or just caught up in the thought of. The once hopeless romantic is slowly becoming heartless can't see clear due to Hidden Heartbreaks.

Hidden Heartbreak

As the saying goes it's better to have love and lost
Then to have never loved at all
Who was it that made that up because?
What it doesn't prepare you for is the emotional fall
Here I am a man scorned
A good man disguised as a bad boy and I can't make sense of it all
Buried under wrecked emotion
That's the suit that I wore
Probably need to change clothes and transform
Instead I take the bullshit to heart see
She said I wasn't well equipped so now I'm ego fucking
Recording me stroking and with no words needed
Her love faces say she's cumming
You didn't like my appearance
You said I didn't fit the image, So changed it up
Skinny jeans, oversized T and some Jordan's is this what you want?
My actions are only to conceal my heartbreak
Masked my lonely feelings underneath a not giving a fuck face
Now it's I got to get her before she gets me
Every relationship begun is a prelude to another break up
I want to fall in love again, but the thought terrifies me
What if she does what she did?
I know don't judge you off previous chics
You're different, give you a chance
But all I see is another beautiful catastrophe through my clouded lens
So, I pretend to never give my heart
I treat relationships like short sleeves and bare arms
Unfortunately, it's unfair to her

But hey,
They say it's better to love and have lost than to never loved at all
So, I'll continue to be a good man disguised under a broken heart
Afraid to love

By this point he was confused, hurt and not sure if he could trust his feelings, though he longed for love. His heart and mind were in different places leaving him confused…..

Confused by love

Seemingly know what I want but, I'm just not ready yet
Still content with chasing the cat
She stays wet, invitation for the long term
I already brought the shirts labeled king and queen but, hold on to them till I find her
Will you love her when the physicality is gone is something, I often wonder
Shallow thoughts more concerned with the shape than the mental space
When her energy alone is a whole vibe
A hopeless romantic self-admitted
Trying to make her, her and her the Misses
My heart is genuine, I struggle to keep feelings in it
Recovery state dealing with pain and love as simultaneous spirits
Distracted by every curve, content with her yet can see myself with a deeper shade of melanin and better figure
Good thing I'm shy shooter and not trigger happy
The type to take shots at every girl that past me
A quality over quantity type
I can't find love, looking under every rock and every pond
Thinking it's simple but, keep getting it wrong
Confused by love obviously I fall in lust.

After another failed relationship the attitude now Fuck LOVE!!!

Fu*& Love

She said,
I'm single as fuck and I curiously asked her why through compliments
You're beautiful and your aura sheer confidence
She said, well
I dated a fuck boy once and since him I been like fuck love
He institutionalized my heart, and punished my feelings for
Had me thinking it was something other than what it was
My response,
So, what if I told you I wanted to help heal your heart
Get lost in a game of connect the dots
Play she loves me, she loves me not
But, cheat as to never have the thought of losing you
Replace those fuck boy tendencies with some well-dressed vows and I do's
See I date with a purpose, no longer down for Mr. Right now
I'm playing for keeps, apply the same pressure on you as you apply to me
Is this something of intrigue worth a conversation over menu
See I still practice chivalry and due to my past failed efforts
Know how to place a woman first
So, take a chance with me allow me to let demonstrate this verse
Actions speak louder than words so let me reverse that feeling you have from
No longer fuck love but, It's fuck him!!

This broken man couldn't seem to conquer love, steady losing to heartbreak, once in for the long term, He now suffered for what he deemed the last time he'd give his heart away. He was going back to his comfort zone, this mentality formed his demise his signature in letters was forever lonely he was committing Love Suicide.....

Suicide Love Letter

This is a suicide note I wrote
To my previous life and favorite love quotes
Fuck love it's just too damn hard
I can't trust my feelings, got blurry vision and can't focus
My single self –love, yeah that bullshit is no longer working
Cliffhanger with a rope I'm hopeless
Scanning Social media sites, likes and hearts for those I want to be with
Secretly in my feelings like how the fuck does he make that work
What the fuck does she see in him?
Looking for reasons; romance surfing
Can't even find temporary purpose during cuffing season
Seems so easy
With all the internet dating and jumping in DM's
Fuck a date, come through Netflix and Chill rendezvous
I'll even get them lemon peppers you like
She responds smiling face, eggplant, splash emoji OTW
On the couch Lemon pepper and Hennessey
Fuck my life, fuck love, fuck her for calling me soft
I open doors caused I raised a gentleman, simply put I'm a chivalrous individual
It's like 1000 to one odds the possibility that I'm single
When he' outright gay and him well he bisexually mingles
I'm walking around celibate with a dry dick hoping my next sexual encounter is the right fit and look at what happens
Nice guys finish last
Meanwhile awe
Look at him with her all happy smiling and laughing #forever love
My struggles with these feelings got me placing slits in my wrist, cocked pistols with rubber grips to my temple
Silencer on so the neighbors don't hear shit.

Lonely is my only company
No woman no cry
#Singleforlife strong arm emoji
This is Love Suicide

Phase II:
The Sex Diaries

Chapter II Introduction (The Sex)

After the numerous relationships and failed experiences
He fell back to the only drug he knew. He began to use sex as a vice,
His new addiction, he'd hide his feelings within erotic stimulation
An attempt to cope with the fact that he may never find what true love is.
He needed a woman but, choose to believe they needed him.
At a point where he was lost, were they using him for the orgasm, his role relegated to simply a nut or was he using them….

Pleasure Box

I felt like pussy was the remedy
Between her legs the battlefield
At war with my BFF and my enemy
No matter what I was going through
Her pleasure box was a reality that was virtual
Simply amazing what her moans could do for a man's confidence
Before entrance pocket prince, after the nut cocky as shit
The feeling of her precipitation was unreal
Submerged, and boxed in
She became another satisfied victim of the orgasm
My temporary sanity
Though often times confused was I
The user or was I simply being used?
Regardless, I can think of no better place to be
Then drowning in the depths of her wetness
30 to 45 minutes of erotic pleasures
My erection leading the search for orgasmic treasure
Increasing my dopamine, her box became my addiction
For her I was a fiend
She assumed the role as my world's immunity
Within her walls I felt nothing, anything outside of that moment was numb to me
She allowed me to see the world different
It was embedded in her center where I learned to use my third eye's vision
She is my muse; a sip of her elixir makes you change your views
Suddenly I believe in me, I can be president too
Seeking answers L-O-V- consumed by obstacles, Desperately in search of love,
Meanwhile, lost in her pleasure box

Misguided and directionless, lacking trust he only allowed himself to feel the physical part of a relationship. It truly became about the sex

Untitled Sex......

The mood is slow jams, candles and incense
Can I ask you a question miss?
Would you allow me the opportunity to turn you out?
Do things to your body you've only read about in erotic novels
I'd like to translate those pages into graphic episodes
Leg shaking spasms, curse words as you explode
Exposing to me your inner most freak
What do you know about a peppermint tongue kiss?
Never in a rush, I'll take my time with it
Start with your lips then taste the rest of you
Get lost midway, her sex candy is so edible
The dialect we speak
The ancient lingo of soul snatchers
This is only the beginning
As I am a true believer of your orgasm before my entrance
A grown man never afraid of assistance
I'll join you in playing with your favorite toy
Ménage trois
Let B.O.B penetrate, while I concentrate on that almond joy center
With your permission over earlobe nipples and whispers
I ask
Are you ready to receive slow, deep inches in various positions?
Let's play a game, called tantric positions
Backshot entrance, cheeks spread to add depth
Apply kisses to your back, hair pulling and ass slaps
Grab you by your neck pull you closer and ask you what's next?
How can I please you?
As I enter from the side, I remind you that you're soaking wet
Missionary gives us that eye contact bringing you closer to orgasm
Submerged in your ocean, focused on delivering deep perfect stroking

Beautiful, how would you like to finish this?
Climb on top but, wait mount my face first
Face the headboard or reverse allow me to quench my thirst
Stroke your joystick, taste my emotions
I want to drown my tongue in your sexual abyss and dependent
upon the level of nastiness may even give that ass a kiss
Now ride your dick, Kegel squeeze arms locked on my chest
Use cuss words for descriptiveness just as you cum
Collapse my love, bite if you want
Leg spasms, this is only round 1

As he figures love is just a four-letter word without meaning,
his drug of choice becomes her orgasm and he chooses to take
explorations in search of. Hoping to shadow his heart from love.
He journeys to a colorful sexual bliss within her walls are a Shade
of Pink…..

Shades of pink

It was said to me that shades of pink
Is what is seen during orgasm
So, I want to explore your standards
Using my pink tongue to trace your leg into your pink walls
Increase the precipitation, allow the release of
Through the breaking of your flood walls
The taste of her juices is delicious, a peach pineapple mango flavored spirit
The reason I keep going as your legs lock, shivering and your hand controls the motion from above
Is I want you to not only see the shades of pink but hear them
This is a lesson that contains onomatopoeia
Starts with clitoral stimulation, slow it down or speed me up
I'm grown and don't fair grab your favorite toy and lay there
We can ménage a trois
There's methods to your legs in V positions, locked under my arms
This way you can't run, only continue to cum
We fill the room up with words like our vocabulary sucks
Shit, damn and you muthafucka
Give you a break for a minute as I softly kiss your earlobe while asking you permission for entrance
Once given I explore the depths of your orgasmic bliss
Inch after hard inch I apply pressure, asking your guidance for the precision stroking
Body movements, heavy breathing
Got it that spot has been noted
My pleasure is giving you pleasure
Ass slaps to acknowledge your efforts, Fuck a favorite lets have sex in origami positions
Make that shit up as we go, just promise me that you'll continue to flow

Leg on my chest, to deepen the stroke my mouth filled with your toes
Hands can be where you want them to be, Pinning you down or aroungd your throat
What I want is to modify Kama Sutra and allow Shades of Pink to display the ambience of our artwork
Cum First, cum with me then cum again

The broken man seeks sanity within her walls, if only for a minute he felt valued, needed
The therapy required to hide his truest feelings. Numb for the moment until his erection and her wetness had subsided. He once again went on a quest to find himself. With her he became lustfully infatuated , watching her walk using his Vivid Imagination…..

Vivid Imagination

Apologies, I hope you don't mind if I write you something a bit nasty
I, often times enjoy visions of you from balcony views
Confession, I have pictured you naked
I got a vivid imagination; my thoughts be running wild
Like Wow!!! I tell myself Calm down
Yet I keep crafting these erotic paintings
My finger tracing your lips before kiss
I'm infatuated with the taste of your Mocha skin
And I imagine it to taste similar to the sweetness of southern bred peaches and Caribbean mangoes
I mentally pretend my tongue is caressing your clit in between vibrated penetrations of your favorite toy
Apply penetration to your G spot in hopes of making you explode
May lay a slap upon cheek, followed by kisses only if you like me to take that course
She has her own name I call her temptation
You, control the penetration,
Tell me the way you like to take it and I'll oblige taking my time in search of what your bodies needs
That place where your toes curl from rotations in between
With you I envision the sex is greater
Masturbating while I eat, conversations between me and your wetness
Having orgasmic confessions from sucking and licking sessions
Come up for air, then ask you a question
Do you like this? No answer
She simply grabs my head and put me back to work
Oh shit, I'm about to …
Exactly the words I want to hear from her , that's my favorite verse
I penetrate slowly and whisper to you while your levies breaking

What's your favorite position?
Slide in inches, each stroke deeper than the first I want the next orgasm to snatch your soul.
Your body leaves the Earth
A Vivid Imagination

After imagining moments with her, He became fixated on her physical worth. Knowing a woman's mind is the primary piece to her orgasm he dedicated himself to her Wettification.

Wettification

This is your wettification
A sexual stimulation to create orgasm
Your legs spasm from my tongue's bad habits
I'm a greedy bastard
I continue to swallow her as she splashes
And her taste is addiction
Her ocean is wet as I enter, filling her love canal with 8.5 hard inches
I whisper "Your love tunnel is ridiculous"
Mouth wide open yet speechless
My hands caress her features as her eyes say it all
You enjoy the perfect stroke
Not too hard, Not too soft
Your desire is that I slide in deep then pause
Hold it right there, don't you move
Creating that perfect melodic blend
Skin to skin, scratching and grabbing anything we can hoping that this moment of passion will never end
Your legs spread wide V-shape, I turn around half push-up half plank
In search of better leverage
This sex isn't average but a wettification
My way of saying thank you
A first-class ticket to ecstasy requiring noon time Deja vu
Positions we've been through missionary, sideways, cowgirl
Now it's for those deep back shots ask for
Ass slaps and hair pulls
You like standing on your tippy toes and throwing it back
So, excited I stop, drop to my knees and have a conversation one on one with your treasure box
Quenching my thirst as I sip on your love juice

Then slide up and reinsert you
The hard reset
You take control, it's your turn
Ride me till you cum
Then slide up my chest, clitoral vibrations reverse the position as you sit it on my face You are now the conductor of 69 ways
The view is great while you use your mouth and heavy spit to caresses my love stick
She is Miss Magna Cum Lata on a full scholarship
And this is your wettification
My way to say thank you

His hidden depression in love sessions treating sex like a game, he studied the art of service, once told he wasn't deserving. The thought plagued him time and time again, not sure if he had enough of the physical gifts, he worked tirelessly to master freaky play …..

Freaky Play

I don't want it if it's not nasty
Disrespect the dick
Lots of spit, hand in a circular motion
Stroking while making those slurping sounds damn
She just sucked the soul right out of me
Her disrespectful ass swallowed every inch
She's turned on by my exotic moans and
She caught of glimpse of me curling my toes
She's soaking wet
My pettiness kicks in, you can't do this to me
So, sit on my face and let's compete
Play a game of freaky you, freaky me
My tongues gentle caress makes you scream
Running is not a possibility that's why I locked my arms around your knees
I make that pussy glisten, applying deep suction to your clitoris
As I switch to licking at different speeds
Your wand ain't got nothing on me
Matter of fact grab your favorite toy and we can tag team
Self-admitting, I cheat use it to double bank
Allow it to explore vices my fingers and tongue can't
He is initial penetration; my tongue continues to taste ya
Call the play, at the line audible stroke and tease
Broken free of your inhibitions you begin to squirt or cream
Then switch positions that's your choice
I'm game for origami
I meant to put it on that way
That make you stop what you're doing mid-day and dream
Call me up like
Shit, fuck you doing to me

Other end like Hi Bae, nothing really, it's simply my pleasure to please
Matter of fact I'm just waiting on you to finish your day so you can come home to me
I miss your taste
Setting up for another game of freaky play

Lost, he would journey to her, looking for comfort, knowing her efforts were only a temporary fix, his complex within himself was that for her he only provided good dick. His efforts were only appreciated when she'd cum in the nighttime but, what lies after…..

Nighttime temptations

I watch her as she sleeps soundly
The image of her thick, curvy physique arouses me
In an attempt to awaken her beauty
I remove skin from sheets and dive headfirst into her booty
Apply kisses, lower back and to each her cheeks
In my mind going through graphic positions
To be her freak
A good student
I learn what she teach
My tongue makes it way down to partial V
Apply sensual massages to her clitoris
Now turned on by her exotic moans, toe curling and hands on head control
As she buries my face in between her legs and drowns me in her sexuality
Body tightens she screams out don't stop I'm cumming daddy
My hardened dick, ready for stimulus I slide my hard love inside her warm wetness inch by inch
Bury my face in her neck and indulge in her erotic scent
Hands interlocked, eye contact as we continue to adventure through positions
Missionary, reverse the rodeo the way her ass bounces on me
Nothing could prepare, I cum as she cums again….

Hating nights alone, he lived in a vicious cycle of moments late nights creeps, the sidepiece, man want to be for only for these moments his life was filled with late nights and Good moaning's….

Good Moaning

I Woke up this morning next to you
Your curves, your skin, you look so edible
The both of us
Skin bare we lye there naked
Erected, you felt it too did that move you know the one
Slide that booty up the fake adjustment
Let me sneak grind up on it, just for reaction
Boy, you ain't sleep
You knew exactly what you were doing when you decided to wear that to bed
Them boy shorts damn, that bare ass now
What happened to them?
The only thing better than breakfast is your soothing wetness
Sex in place of coffee
Helpless to your bidding, lured in, sweet kisses applied
To awaken the vision
She's a stomach sleeper, so my tongue caresses your spine
Kissing both cheeks, one at a time
Spread' em, I dive in and speak poetry in a French dialect
Your hips begin to rotate tracing out the contours of my face
You follow the wave in Caribbean rhythms
Room is filled with the sensual sounds of sex from inches delivered
Allow me now to feed you breakfast
Turkey bacon, vegetable omelets, fruit cups and Mimosas
Good Moaning

Living in the moments of lust, going from woman to woman, no trust in himself. He was broken but her pleasure box was the fix. In that moment, love was almost possible as he created intimate spaces to hide his feelings in creating Another Nasty Jawn ….

Another Nasty Jawn

See, just like the perfect picture
The delivery of the dick is about angles
We link up, and we fucking like strangers
Momentarily hating love
You mad at him, I'm mad at her
Conversations leads to penetration
My tongue caressing your walls
The orgasmic eruption that fills the room
It's like the heavens opened the gate when I'm inside of you
Deep, heavy breathes to your neck
You are soak and wet
My penetration is the perfect dissemination
As you enjoy every inch
The motion your hips to the rhythm
You want to catch the dick at the perfect depth, with the perfect grip
Position switch, devils arch your back I grab your hips before strokes applied
I deliver a Thank you kiss
Smack you on that ass, the motion is God's gift
On edge from mouth to clit kiss, I slide in dick
Spread the cheeks, one leg up
So, I can go deep
Grab both arms, pull you back towards me
We both finish with those oh fuck screams

If only he applied as much time to healing as he did to his coaxing vices, he may have found one with the potential to spend the rest of his life with. He'd hold decent conversations with pleasure in mind. Often, giving way to the ambience. A man's deepest secrets can be found buried inside his walls if only they talked

Walls talk

If these walls could talk
They'd snitch on what we do behind closed doors
Like how you exit the shower and my tongue becomes your towel
How I talk to you in vowels like AEIOU an orgasm
Cum smother my face
I'll indulge in the taste and won't waste a drop of your candy-coated ecstasy
Sex with me is amazing and we got chemistry
Your pussy is the key to my freak
Your nakedness has me lost in your sexuality
Your booty bouncing strategies
Small shorts reveal the perfect amount of cheek
Teasing and distracting me
You got a thing for that shit
Fuck this game, they suck anyway
I want to play with you
Run my tongue down your spine then slide and explore inside you
Watch your movements to the orgasmic rhythm and release that freak
See there is no holding back I want you to know it's me
Stimulus and pure bliss as these walls talk about how you climax
Grabbing sheets, arched back and how I reach my pinnacle as you ride atop of me
Your Words "You like this pussy?"
My response in between deep breathes "Yes"
If these walls could talk they'd tell all our secrets

Running around with multiple partners, never finding intimacy. He was Mr. hit and run, nothing more than the physical flesh, he delivered the nut. Deep inside wishing secretly to himself that she was the one. The words left untold of romantic episodes he'd go on a search to taste the rainbow.....

Taste the Rainbow

Face submerged in your pineapple passion fruit
Drowning in the taste of your love juice
My pleasure is watching your love faces
The leg shaking vibrations from the clitoral stimulation
My tongue becomes your Hitachi replacement
You, running away screaming wait
Heavy breathing as my tongue enjoys the taste
Delicious finger licking entrees turned desert dependent on positions
I present to you your throne, your crown the orgasm
Patiently waiting for you to place it on
Hard work is my gift to you, I want you on my face
Smother me while I grab your waistline
Enjoy this ride, let your juices saturate
Applying moisture to this beard of mine
I want my tongue to glide and trace while you're bent over
I'm admiring both smiles, ass slapping and licking
Arms wrapped around your waist
Just in case you were planning to escape
I'll only let you go after you cum and I need at least two of them
Now lay on your back legs in a V shape
Your hands on my head controlling the tempo and speed
Your clinching up signals to me you're about to bust
Yelling fuck as that body endures that second orgasmic rush
Your love fruit has the sweetest juice
A blend of mango and papaya fruits
That third one got you in a fetal position
Excuse me sweetness, did you forget that I also brought dick?
My tongue has tasted the treasures, now did you want me to put it in?

A hopeless romantic, turned heartless. The pleasure principle made him numb, suicidal feelings for love he never wanted to feel it again. In retrospect he also had no desire to hurt anyone. What he brought to the table was a good time, a friend with benefits, he was a stress reliever

Stress Reliver

She had a long day
Enter the door
Her purse hits the floor
I'll apologize for it later
Dinner, is already made
As I pinned you up against the wall
Kisses applied from my lips to yours
Leg wrapped around my waist
I slip my tongues attention to slide down between your hips
The fact you're already wet
Means you got my mid-day sext
I can't wait to see you, get you undressed
I want to taste how day went
Assist you in reaching that orgasmic bliss
Bath water running
I escort you to it
Favorite wine and playlist over a candlelit ambience
Relax while I prepare your plate
Conversations about your day
Mentally prepare you to stimulate
Me, I serve as a stress reliver, her daily escape
Dry you off, place you on the bed in your favorite position
Apply massage, half naked my shirt is already off as I
Lower my head below your waist,
Legs placed one on shoulder, One flat
See, your toes curl better when you're relaxed
As I prepare to taste your day
Your hands holding my head forcing the focus
Directing the passion, and angles that I play
Lights, camera, orgasm
We are now two pornographic actors delivering a classic performance

The arch of your lower back in my hand is amorous
As my tongue applies suction to your clit
Don't run, cum, enjoy the feeling of orgasms
Then I'll follow it up with some more dick
That plate was ready, you can eat it later.

A thief in the night, never stayed long was more comfortable being in and out of her life. Ducking and dodging any possible feelings for. Simply wanted to temporarily make love in the night and be gone in the morning time good night, good morning

Good Night/Good Morning

She's one in before my entrance
Calculated penetration that stimulates
Positions, we explore Kama Sutra in search of vacations
All expenses paid as we enjoy the tantric waves
Your body precipitates as you ride your daddy till your legs shake
Reaching the edge of insanity
I have become your favorite fantasy
Our bodies explode in volcanic eruptions
Slide that wet, up my chest and sit it on my face
A queen's throne, I breathe you in
The pheromone aroma as my tongue begins licking
Alphabet sex
Finding my way through navigation your orgasmic center
I get lost within the anatomy of your seduction
This is a situation about those oooh- aaah sounds and love faces we making
Headboard shaking as it supports the stimulation
If desire has a flavor, it would be you
Let me bend you over and enjoy the view
Though your favorite position, this is more for me than you
The thickness is remarkable
Don't hold back, smack the mattress, grab the sheets
All that ass please throw it back on me
We compete in a game of who's going cum first?
I'll play wide receiver
Run a precise route and I got great hands
Your position tight end, the quarterback's best friend
Hardest to guard on the field
She is always open to exploring morning orgasms before work
Her preference deep routes down the seam

Wide open as we both deeply breathe upon completion, breakfast, repeat !!!

Holidays was when he found himself the loneliness, wanting her lips to kiss
Her smile to see as she began to open gifts, filling her with excitement however, This Christmas was very different

This Christmas

Twas the night before, but this Christmas is different
Both of us in the mood for giving surrounded by Christmas spirit
The past irrelevant, all about the present and future
Chestnuts roasting on an open fire, hot cocoa, candlelight and marshmallows
The Mistletoe perfectly placed
You, them red cheeky boy shorts with the lace perfectly wrapping your gifts
Exposing just enough of that beautiful skin
As you walk, I really believe that reindeers fly and elves exist
Enjoying the walk away while imagining how good you taste
Fellatio vision, my tongue caressing your clitoris
Nasty, lots of spit I want that diamond glistening
Creating orgasmic stimulation, after body shaking you return the favor
No need for silent nights
I prefer loud, exotic moans, climbing the walls and that shit we talk
Sipping eggnog, picturing a white Christmas the beauty of the image
We stand cozily by the window, watching the snow fall
Fireplace trickling, our favorite hallmarks on
Knowing my greatest blessing is simple; within your presence
My unwrapping of you makes up for Santa never answering my letter
It's her chimney I want to slide in, laying in between her legs is comparison to the heavens
Room filled with cinnamon and candy cane scents
Jingle bells, silver and gold that's code for great sex , curling of the toes and that Frosty
I can't move after reaching orgasm pose
Home alone, not this year

This Christmas will be different
Specially you, Special to me.
Good old Saint Nick

Ego shattered and hurt, he used her and knew it. No intents to ever commit. He was broken and in fear of relationships. Would rather live his life as the sidepiece, Mr. tonight

Tonight

Tonight, I made plans for you
Dick on delivery
The keep her wet challenge
The how many strokes does it take for her to erupt in orgasm
Uncontrollable shakes and spasms
Backshots, hand in hand with mattress
Headboard grabbing for leverage
Legs up on my shoulders as you pull me in, then push me out
Eye contact as I place your areola in my mouth
Free hand rubbing clit while I give her inch after hard inch
I want to ensure the penetration takes you places
That in between passionate breathes
I reach the expectations
That only exist in your imagination
Yes, I want to drive your crazy nut after hard nut
Give you dick then massage wetness with my tongue
I want to unleash the slut in you
Me, her and you a private rendezvous
Meet the freak, use your mouth and taste yourself as I come up hands free
Now kiss me
How nasty do you want to be?
Tonight, I made plans for you

Though he went through with the plans to heal temporarily, he was still lost in search of love. Lost, fighting his own ego he was tired of only being a good time. He wanted to find that one and please her. Stuck could only be her pleasure.

Pleasure(Please her)

Last night I saw you
And I thought of every possible origami position
She deserves this dictation
Love faces and orgasms
Splash pools and shaking
Innovative ways to create the spaces; Use your imagination
Your heavy breathing is the signal of anticipation
Tongue tracing prior to the penetration
I offer deceptive depthness as I'm experienced, a master in using leverage
Sex is so much better with me, than with them young boys who didn't know what to do with you
Drilling fucks, screwing you
Hopping in and out of your box abusing you
My efforts precision, aimed at pleasing you
I listen to the things your body tells me to do
That's the playbook
Your love faces the applause for crowd participation
Let's adventure to Ménage a trois… you, me, tongue and your favorite toy
Pick it rabbit or the wand, hell we can switch it up
It'll be fun to bring you joy
I want to excerpt every effort to stimulate your pleasures
Get lost in your treasures, dive in searching or applying pressure

Though often hurt and in his feelings. Sex was his healing or so he thought. Rather than talk it out and heal he'd rather hide his problems. His attitude she doesn't care anyway, she's only concerned with the orgasm. So his feelings lie dormant, unhealed yet submerged.

Submerged

Lately been sipping that brown
Hennessey chronicles of making sweet love
Extra mannish shit like
Lay there with your favorite toy penetrate and I'll compliment
Submerged
Tongue goes in first
Licking the sweet taste of your excellence
B.O.B strokes you in and out
My tongue caresses your clit same time, no cheating this is orgasmic foreplay
You cum first before my erection enters
I want to bury your body within the sheets like you're a sexual sacrifice
Let the mattress eat you up, I'll get jealous
Each stroke, one step closer to you levee breaking
You place arch in your back while I apply wet kisses
Hands on your waist you throw it back like you know exactly how you want this dick
Switch positions
On your side, you bend one leg up and I'm an opportunist
I live for indulging in deep conversations
Body talk, submerged in you

Though the conversations ended up being about everything except sex, he even decided to pick one and make a date an erotic trip

Erotica

Lately been sipping that brown
Hennessey chronicles of making love or we can fuck
It's completely up to us
That extra mannish shit like
Lay there with B.O.B.
Menage a trois featuring toy, tongue and dick
Start off with the penetration you control the tempo originally
As I watch and learn your bodies wants and needs
My tongues applies soft caress as compliment
Tongue goes in first, I thirst to taste your sweet excellence
A fast learner, I slowly take over B.O.B. strokes
In, spin and slide it out, taste yourself, see why I act like that
You taste like obsession
Tongue caresses your clit at the same time as B.O.B
You reach and feel the Hard
Now fiending for my entrance but,
No cheating I want that orgasmic foreplay
Show me that fuck face as you grab for the real thing and insert hard love into soft bay
I want to bury your body within the sheets like the bed desires a sexual sacrafice
Let the mattress eat you up
Each stroke, brings you one step closer to your levies breaking; that second nut
Switch positions she says missionary is boring
You place an arch in your back, Hands on your waist "hold on to me" and you throw it back like your life depended on it and you truly know what good dick is
Switch positions again side bends, one leg up and I'm an opportunist and live indulging in deep conversation.

Understanding the power he has, as she does in between her legs, injured heart and he is too quick to give up no longer in search of love just a nut. Her orgasm has become his sanctuary. His strongest efforts are given not to emotional healing but, to good dick delivery.....

Good Dick

Though She may not admit it good dick makes her do things
9 inch and Stroke right makes her a bit cra cra
On the edge of insanity, she start thinking
maybe I can change him ignoring your best friends warning that
he ain't shit but, hard dick and bubblegum
lady going crazy with that good quality dick
Originally, you didn't want kids now you want to have them for him.
Got you like Fuck this nigga, is what you constantly saying half delirious
Hoping if you repeat it over and over again you'll start to believe it
Till his hard love fills your box again creating orgasm
Provided comfort to your G spot
While you Call him daddy
Good dick can be stronger than 90's nose candy
Fuck up her psyche
Got her losing it, seeing illusions of him and another bitch
But, you on the phone with him and he chilling at the crib
Awaiting your arrival to get up in your ribs
Although he did borrow your care once or twice and can't explain his whereabouts
He came back and hit you with that gift good dick
sometimes the difference in you being single and, in a relationship,

Every man has a bad night, however no one ever seems to discuss when a woman's sexual energy is off, and the man leaves with regrets….

Regrets

Excuse Miss lady
I hate to bother you but, I left something last night at the crib and was wondering
Can I get that dick back?
I only ask cuz you really didn't deserve it and I didn't listen to the right head besides the outfit you wore was perfect
This dick shouldn't been free, So please pay me what you owe matter of fact scratch that just give me a refund on my service
Reverse the roles, you should've back paged me
This morning you made me throw out my Hennessey, mixed with the Patron shots had me non observant and I rendered you a service
That left me dissatisfied; The sex was boring and unfulfilling
Shit, I can see why you single
All those physical attributes and you just lay there
If you wasn't into me, then we shouldn't have went there we both could've kept on our clothes, scroll through our phones and ended up with those "OMG Bitch I hate you, Muthafucka I hate you too moans."
So I ask politely,
Can I get that dick back?
It was a mistake simply based off time, place and liquor infused drinks.
Maybe conversation was great or shit it was just a bad day
That girl is crazy which normally means the sex is retarded however comma Outside of the physcialities that inspired thee there in no attraction between us
We simply fucked, woke up.... shit we didn't even do brunch
I left the crib, didn't even want to wash
So excuse me miss cuz ummm
Your name I forgot
Can I get that dick back

Signed,
Mr Looking for love in all the wrong places

After searching in these places he realized he wasn't playing for keeps, rather in the role of temporary. He decided if he was the sidepiece he would at least teach. He fired a warning shot…..

Warning shot

A hopeless romantic
All alone on love street
Ego shattered as I come to realization that she is not for me
Her house hold is with he
My role, that of the sidepiece
Acquired that by her hip tease
I accepted it wholeheartedly now I walk around on a leash
Only called upon for her pleasure release
As, agreed I would never destroy a household
But, Walk around in an apartment with slippers and house robes
Real comfortable, Mr I ain't shit
I live the theme written by Joe
All the things your man won't do
Deep strokes and choke holds
But most notably I simply listen to you
Cultivated her love language
Know that she speaks in terms of a complicated passionate endearment
Never straightforward, She hints towards it
You know her better than me
You used to listen for it
Problem is you got comfortable, started practicing complacency
So, when you left your house, she gave me a copy of the keys
You left the door open for me
All I need is a crack
I've had my heart shattered in the past
This is the petty get back
She's the beautiful woman in the world from a distance
I only have her temporarily
Orgasms from various angles and positions
Her heart resides with you, yet she is left wishing

For old time's sake
God forbid if you find out it's properly on site
I figure chances worth taking
Since my heart was forsaken
Strike year I'll be the replacement
Mistakes I've made in the past repeated
She's told me constantly, over and over again
He just doesn't listen to my outcries, and you hear me
So, I take advantage
Intimate dances in the nude
I treat her special, to you its disrespectful
Yet I respect you
Which is why
I'm a hopeless romantic
All alone on love street
Ego shattered as I come to realization that she is not for me

He'd seemingly given up on love, replacing the empty feeling of a broken heart with a temporary fix , It became his drug, often times leaving him confused. Her body became a need no longer a want. He healed internal wounds through her orgasm. Exotic moans of OMG was his art

OMG

Wet kisses applied to your skin
This is the foreplay
Prequel before I attempt to blow your mind
Roll you over, smacking ass cheeks as I pull the panties down
My tongue caresses your spine
Sweet whispers, in between ear nipples
Reminding you that you're fine and I appreciate this opportunity with you
To perform orgasmic spasms, now back down I slide
Tongue in position to taste that passion fruit
So, turned on and a little nasty I might just eat the booty too
Fuck it I want to turn you out
Taste your pleasure in hopes that you squirt the flavor out
Soaking wet and one orgasm in before penetration
Eight inches slow and deep filling you up
Hip grabbing wet as I hold on
Equestrian horse
Then you throw me off and taste yourself, now you see why I'm crazy
Backshots holding your arms so you can't run from me
Bend you over the bed, one leg up and spread cheeks
From these angles those 8 inches feel like 16
You screaming fuck I'm bout to cum again
Now I drop down to knees and taste your cream
Lay you on your back apply tongue massage to nipples then grind
Missionary   till we pass out
Next morning, arise again to sex, coffee and bacon

As he awakens to the sunrise, he realizes once again he's served as Mr. one night, though parts of him wanted to be in love in with her she told him no feelings involved. That this was a fictional reality simply a moment. It was just sex

Just Sex

It's just sex
It really means nothing
Backshots, no facial expressions needed cause we was only fucking
No relationship
Never even explored one
We both agreed it was just about the orgasm
Pinned down emotions as If they were wrist
An ambience is overrated
When only physical needs exist
Kisses applied without intimate lips
Meaningless, only to pacify vagina passage
Her spit on the dick, not signature nastiness
Just disrespect maybe towards him yet, I reap the benefits
No signs of love making outside of song lyrics
We never had such a pleasurable experience
Our naked eye appearance
Was wet pussy and hard dick sealed with toxicities kiss
That's the example we grew up with
Followed up by our own failed relation trips
What do you get
Mr. I ain't shit meets Queen Boss Bitch
So, that childhood game that went
Sitting in the tree K-I-S-S-I-N-G is now irrelevant
As adults it more like this
Hands on the headboard for leverage
She's gripping the sheets, legs in a V
Testing out bed springs F-U-C-K-I-N-G
It's just sex
Stimulated penetrations without feeling
Stroking without emotions
For that search of love, we repeatedly come up hopeless
Given up on the trusting the heart
Replacing it with body parts

Phase III:
Life Writing Diaries

Chapter III Introduction (Life Writing)

The world today is different, as we live amongst a pandemic, entanglements is the new word for side loving. There is also the dominate issue of mental health, Gun violence is at an all-time high, as we culturally express our 1st Amendment right for change. Those that protect and serve society have been exposed for their abuse of power and even the next generation of leaders are in danger as we destroy the schools in which we teach lessons. Return of the unhooded Klansman while Black Lives Matter, we still can't breathe.

Letter to the King
(Dedication to DaeQuan my Son)

What do you say to your heart? Please continue to pump blood for me
What do you say to a lung? Please continue to breathe
Son, they attempted to take away your royalties, but young man please know that you're are a KING
They said his hair was of wool and skin of bronze
Which means you are the image of God
But son be warned your melanin is a threat
9 times out of 10 you're guilty until proven innocent
Because they want you to believe that your skin is a sin and that due to it's the darkened tint you should have a less than complex
Though you were suburban born and raised, never played in the projects hallways because that was part of my duty was to ensure that
Son, know that your complexion is blessed by God, for it is sun-kissed
So, go outside, be great but play safe
I can't control the reaction to a hoodie and skittles mindset
Son,
Please know to enjoy the process towards the progress
See success comes with haters, Don't be easily frustrated
Our journey has been from kings to slavery our bloodline is double AA positive
Adapt and adjust
Then give the knowledge back that's how we start the legacy
See they'd rather you save keep your money gain with low interest rates, when they invest
Then give trust funds and inheritance to their kids
My son,
Ignore their racist dialect don't give them the energy

Carry this shield and sword with you, fight off their apparent ignorance
Know that everything valuable was first created black
You are part of history, covered up publicly as its part of a system they use to control you
Son,
They hate your greatness, funny how they depend on you to be lazy
Yet we came from slavery, see hard work is hard work
Educate yourself show them respect until it's lost
Commit to your net worth, cuz they play a game of money talks
Most of all remember your skin alone is the threat, To hear you roar the world is not ready yet
You are king

Queendom (Message to Alliyah my daughter)

Dear Love,
You were born with a crown on your head, Being a Queen is your birthright
Know that wearing a crown is heavy and not light
Since day one my teachings have been brains over beauty
Cuz you gotta keep your mind right
Your 14 now and I am still trying to hold on to your childhood ways for dear life
Protect you from this world that looks to rob you of your innocence
Make your skin a sin and use your figure for its benefits
Kidnap you and force you to play victim.
See not only do you have to deal with the same inequalities of woman but, you were born with brown skin
Placed in a world of double standards where you gotta hustle harder than HIM.
Listen love you can be whatever it is you feel and you will, as long as you keep a close eye out for those with bad intentions
They'll question your intelligence, play you as a something just to look at
Curly hair, natural curves you can think your moms for that
Baby Girl,
The world is going make it hard for you, expect you to quit and be an Instagram model
Listen, always remember your significance and know within you lies the strength of 1,000 sisters.
Remember I fathered you, aligned the stars, sun, Earth and the moon
On bended knee, eyes closed, in prayer and faith I carved you
Instilled deep within you the ancestral strength of Makeda, Candance and Amina
That's warrior blood, beauty and queendom

So that radiates off your perfect complexion, Study your historical lessons in them you will find the your essence.
Don't be so distracted by Instagram likes and Youtube
It's fine for that quick hit but don't be consumed boo; truth of the matter is they make their money while undercutting you.
The system has created this distraction and you have a Queendom to rule
Even though you are the center of a family tree don't be fooled by fraudulent dudes
You should assist in building him and he should do the same for you
Be critical of the conversation even more so his moves
See baby,
Relationships come with complications, at times they going get a little messy, Boys can be a distraction
So, I recommend you take care of your professional and personal matters
Before making a family plans because its mommas' baby, daddies maybe it's no guarantee he'll stick around
Besides, you got plenty of time and don't make the mistake to be financially tied cuz men look at favors differently; Your body is a temple of Egyptian imagery
Be good with you before leaning on him, keep your self-esteem high because as flawed men we will try to ruin it
Never give any man or woman your dignity or self respect.
Grind hard and go get it yourself, do not be impressed by what is simply materialistic
Ask what's behind the closed door? Meaning what's really within him
He'll call you stuck up, selective names, may even say your daddy messed you up

Those are signs boo that he's not the one for you, if you really want to slick talk him
Calmly ask him would he want his daughter to be with a man like you? Then walk off
Baby girl
You got to watch the way you dress; unfortunately, I can't control it and you will be judged by that.
You're born into a system that doesn't want to see you progress
Male dominated industries, not ready to call the CEO Miss a continuous fight for equal pay and politics.
Just know that the struggle is real as a black woman, You are the strongest of the sexes
See God made men first, took a rib and carved your perfection.
You're not physically stronger so you gotta outthink them.
Remember, You can never lose as long as you learn the lesson taught, that's the win.
Above all remember daddy will love you through it.
See, being a Queen is your birthright but, to bear the crown is a heavy task not light.
I LOVE YOU!!

The Message

Look at me king
I am everything that I shouldn't been. Young, Black and Gifted
The embodiment of all that you didn't want me to be
I am the results of the experiment
You placed me in the project, as a project
The variable X to your constant and off my bronze melanin reflects greatness
I dissipated the hatred, took your low income status of oodles and noodles babies and navigated using Octane 93 so thanks for the fuel that drives me
I do admit your experiment was successful in snatching away those that look like me
Taking away the father faces
Leaving Momma with some hardships however, you didn't realize that the black woman is a goddess, so her strength, god send.
Translation the black family she "Got It"
Told me Son, in you lies the heart of a lion, your bloodline is King
Crowm me for I exude royalty
Use that pen to author your own destiny and since I haven't suffered from writers block in a while
Everyday I rise, I was taught I had to stare death in the eyes
Good thing for me that my horus is scoped in
Allowing the building of mental pyramids to oversee the box you trying to put me in
The hidden ignorance because Black lives matter when it's convenient politics
Jurors deciding the value of my death, last breath taken while sitting in the crib
Playing xbox with my only, I guess the surround sound of Gears of War sound dangerous
Mr Lawman how does this, my defenseless death only equate 5 years

The same distribution of 50 marijuana kilograms
I thought it was justice for all, but it's JUST US depenent upon financial status and the pigment of your skin
The irony that a hooded black man breeds fear, When it was a Grand Master hooded man with a badge that came up with it
I am a threat due to the color of my skin yet originally thought of as 3/5 of a man I guess that evolution
You use the 2nd Amendment right for mass murder justification
Yet I'm blackballed cuz I choose not to stand for the anthem, and the original reason why appears long forgotten
Place pen to pad is what my momma said
Use your words, and platforms given to elevate them
Left hand Marcus Garvey, Right hand Huey Newton
10- point programs but, maintain your swagger float like a butterfly sting like a bee
Fulfill those thought to be lucid dreams by any means
Release the hieroglyphic symbology's and strategies to get ahead within your speech
Always give them a message. Your intellect is the greatest weapon

Meant to Heal (Mental Health)

As I stare at this man in the mirror
His image says that he is in search of healing
Whether it's from the anxiety, depression or the Post traumatic slave syndrome
He feels lost
In a world where his gender and skin complexion alone
Has him guilty for cause, fighting for support
With a low percentage of receiving and innocent verdict
His blackness is a victim to the corrupt prison system
Raised by a single parent so, in all relationships he now shoulders these burdens
A man is raised to believe that his feelings aren't important
He needs to bottle up his emotions and focus
Or have his masculinity left open to questions
They say a man isn't supposed to cry
Well, I am broken today
Scattered thoughts I dilute them with Hennessy
No ice, no chaser, I'll take mines straight
I'm simply searching for a substance that'll temporarily heal me
Take away the internal pain
I got emotions, left undiagnosed because of.my melanin tied in with that man's strength complex don't allow me to express
So, with this mentality how can I communicate to her clearly
And then if I open up, increased possibilities that she'll call me soft
As a man I have never been able to balance being hard with being in love
These are just a few things that might ruin the relationship before it even starts
Add that to the fact I'm already going in with a broken heart and zero examples of what a healthy relationship was
A shattered ego and sidepiece complex meaning

I never think that I'm the only.one, not quite enough for her
Which is the answer to my question of why I'm so aggressive
At times appearing to be jealous
I am lost, I am broken
I am a black man in search of mental health
I to am men-to-heal

Battles I

A formidable opponent
the dilemma got you feeling as though you can't win
Well trained, no days off
Sneak in your thoughts, projecting white noise
Tainted confidence
Lost, no voice screaming loud
Filled with clouds of doubt
Notional ideologies of the impossible odds
On bended knee, spirit given to God
As the enemy looks back at you
Same height, same skin complexion
That mirror reflection and enemy is you

Battles II

Moving motionless
Filled with a sense of hopelessness
Though I've been known to devise thought provoking shit
I'm slowly losing focus, lost of confidence
Forgot my own worth
shit
Internally, discussing inadequacies when I should be totally believing in me
Trust the process yet struggle to trust myself
Anxiety and stress
Got me thinking my life is a mess
Though God both blessed and gifted me,
The devils pursuing my idle mind and playing with my consciousness
Truth be told I struggle mentally
In disbelief that this man in the mirror is me
Sometimes the evil in me is released instead of combating
It merges with the blood of the beast and makes its way to the surface
Thoughts like you ain't shit and nugga you're worthless
I mean think about it
If you die today you wouldn't even be missed, your life has no purpose
Give it to me
The devil is pulling on my feelings
Got me....
Bended knee praying harder for clarity
I am a lost child Jesus please bring me home
Help me understand your plan, I need desperately to see
Amen!

Broken Mirror

As a black man I was told never to cry
Never show your emotions, that's masculinity suicide
I Never asked questions, simply found truth in those lies
So, in turn for years I've bottled up my feelings, Sided with foolish pride
Never talked them out, I done Damn near lost my mind
Due to my own ignorance I couldn't see the signs
It's been the consequence of many relationships and to those ladies I apologize
If I can't talk out my feelings, How the fuck can I express them
I struggle to sleep and with belief in self, inadequacies feeling like I'm just not enough.
Excuse me can you lend me your ear just for a sec
I simply want to discuss with you the state of my mental health
I want to get better simply lost and seeking direction
Which way do I go to express confession and what about what I was told?
I know that you're busy, in a rush but I ask for nothing just for you to listen
And if you choose to stay and not walk off you just might make a difference
This may be this conversation that keeps me in good spirits
I'm broken and looking for a reason to not go on living
To foolish to see my blessings, as unhappiness is my new normal
I got a pocket full of pills and a pint of liquor in my pocket
.38 special snub nose that I play Russian roulette with and already 4 shots in
Suicide letter is already written for my kids.
See in my mind, if I die, I become an angel for them.
Baby moms forever anyway claimed I won't shit, so now I'm omnipresent

A black man broken is easily provoked and that makes him dangerous
God forgive if I don a hoodie and me and my cell phone have a tight grip
6 o'clock news boys in blue interview, he approached the officers with a weapon
I just want to discuss my mental health as I have a twisted perception
I can no longer deal on my own with the anxiety and depression
This world don't love me, who's going miss me anyway?
I picture my funeral empty
Dressed in sweat pants and a white tee
Outside of my own momma no one there to talk or identify me
I am a broken mirror of a black man
Hidden beneath the belief of masculinity
Look at me King!!!
I am a broken mirror of me

Mass Eulogy

I was at a party and a semi-automatic weapon took my life
I went to school this morning but, didn't return home that night
Now I lay me down to sleep, I pray the lord my soul you'll keep
I rest soul wide awake, watching my loved ones shed tears for me
Forced to wonder about your second amendment
It makes the US billions, the right to bear arms we get it
However, somewhere after the "well-regulated militia" the meaning got lost
What's the price on the head of the victims? Is it worth the loss of children?
Those tax paying civilians, guess cuz I'm lower to middle class for me it wasn't written
When the emotionally enraged simply load and spray; scream mental health issues then they get away
Signs were there, they were cra cra before we sold them weaponry
They say bullets have no names, that's no longer the case just look at the list of 308 blood stained
No more joyful laughs and happiness only pain for those families
We call them tragedies, yet with no means to an end it will only happen again
AK-47s with war magazines available for purchase, easier to get than increased credit limits
My god in heaven, please use me as a spiritual weapon to unmask the deception within 5 pounds of pressure as in Isiah 54: one seven your words state "No weapon formed against you shall prosper, And every tongue which rises against you in judgment You shall condemn."
Bury them and allow their soul eternal rebirth in damnation
America eliminate the semi-automatics and save this nation.

Who Shot ya…

Why did you shoot my brother
That's the question I ask the gun that took his life
Why were you so accurate, why not misfire that night
We're so embattled with the actions of Colin Kaepernick let's
revisit the reason behind the knee in the first place
The biased treatment. The Unfair court case
The police brutality when they're paid to protect me
Yet, my black or brown melanin is somehow a weapon
Sirens, lights, hand ups might be my last days
Yet all the shootings and beatings go on daily and the system looks away
Why do you fear my strength, I bleed that same as you
My ancestors came enslaved, in chains then broke away
So laws were established to control me, separate me from my family
Use TV to depict me as a violent threat, a visually genius concept
He shot me because I reached for ID but, he told me, He shot me
with claims I was resisting arrest when in fact I only wanted the
answer to a question I asked,
He shot me because I was security,
He shot me in my own apartment
Nothing has been done as of yet so I no longer question them it
must be the guns fault for my death

You Go Girl

All she's posting is gym pics of curved perfection
Her secret weapon a great diet and limited stressing
Left him on read and didn't seek closure
Took away his chances to come over and exploit your emotions
You Go girl
She working on her glow up
Was professional before you showed up
Now sprints and squats that progress she's leveling up
At your expense you trying to ignore her but, ya man He keep liking all her pics
Got you In her inbox and DM's just to drop a quick text
Secret apologies that have zero effect
No acknowledges from his big eye emojis, Aight she petty maybe a quick thumbs up check
You got curved to the left, shook that your pipe game you pride yourself on might just be average
To the table you didn't bring anything else, see you didn't turn her out but, and forgot that it's the mind of a woman that drives the passion in her body parts
Your disloyal and non-commitment actions turned her savage
Now she's Ms. Murder body, like her body actually catches a body
They shooting, made you look.
WTF? In her in box
Claimed she didn't do that when ya'll was together
Well nugga you didn't let her, never consistent on bettering her efforts instead of calming her you brought the stressing and yet and still she adjusted it try to love you
Then you disrespected, triggered her De ja Vu
Instead of mending a broken heart she's now like fuck him too
She knows her worth and you didn't define the value
You Go Girl.

Celibacy

This celibacy shit
Got me going crazy, like I'm extra thirsty
Completely dehydrated
I mean basic conversation turned into reasons for masturbation
My imaginations enjoying the way her lips move on her face
Appears to be preciperatation
Damn she thick in them yoga pants when before I never noticed it
Easily stimulated I gotta practice window shopping and don't
touch it,
leave the crack alone
Celibacy
Got me seeing things like Asian woman with ass, there's no way
she's carrying that
Shawty phat
I'm extra horny, like Viagra pill popped and two hours past
At the gym watching her run on the treadmill and her sweat called me
Day 258 and I'm aggressive as hell like I really woke up mad
I miss the taste, it's embedded in my memory
I bet when I finally get some the smell of it probably makes me cum
Premature ejaculation
Celibacy

Digital

This digital age of communication got our minds twisted
Like we can't be who we are, so we attempt to cover up flaws with filters
Use to have to have to throw hands for respect now they use Twitter fingers to call you out
Then we get in our feelings need therapy
Therapist packed cuz we judging self-esteem off likes, angles and hashtags
Just bragged yesterday about the bag, now today I'm trash all based off the outfit I wear
Tagged #lookinglikeyesterdaya#$
Why can't we get it's a screen and some fingers nothing to do with the spirit
Use to be that "stick and stones may break my bones but words will never hurt"
It's the thirst for attention that has some feeling inadequate now all of sudden she need thicker lips , wider hips and her waist snatched #notabasicbi*&^, #sheslimthick
His beard fake, eyes ain't shaped like that, profile reads 6'5 when he's 5'6" then to top it all off he photoshopped the grey sweats package #catfish #MCM
Perfection doesn't exist in the selfie stick, stop letting it ruin your image
Be who you are, God made you beautiful accentuate those features
Allow the world to love your treasures and fuck the Joneses, if you ain't there don't do it to feel pressured
We took a networking and building process and made it opportunistic to reach out and be petty
Misery loves company so they scroll through timelines trying to find a stress outlet

DM/inbox some BS comment without actual concept, In hopes for a response back #StephenASmith
Then they believe it, feel the need to defend self #fightback
Prolly, didn't really mean it comes off the fingers different than the tongue but, we do it for views and likes thinking #virallife
Hell is a cyber bully anyway simple fix
Unfriend or block the hate
Oh, my bad you lose followers that way that may not even know you in real life.

Ms. Beautifully Complicated / The woman

It's her independence that hinders my ability to love her
Injured heart she won't let me in, can't trust the love of man outside of her dad and
That is if she doesn't have issues with him
A failed previous relationship got her making protected judgments restraining and categorizing me as him
Can't say I'm different so, I show her such
Her reply still "I'm emotionless"
Confused with what she wants missing the perfect balance
Ms. Independent, fuck a man I got it
She got her own and makes it known every conversation its stated about her master's degree enroot to the PHD in psychology
Seemingly she's over analytically thinking the situation, I'm simply applying chivalry and gentleman behaviors
Open a door I'm too soft, buy you drink and conversate I'm too basic
Miss beautifully complicated
What you arguing for, you big mad or nah
You wanted to be the boss, fell and I'm right here to pick you back up
I'm struggling with communication but, don't have mind reading superpowers
I guessed wrong you wanted consonants and I gave you a vowel
Ms. Beautifully Complicated,
No need for a man and it's clearly stated
"Boy Bye" I got B.O.B at home and no desire for dating
My patience is thin, I dislike being single but, lowering my standards and giving second chances to unworthy men, when all ya'll the same lie, cheat and steal? Why waste time
She's broken from the first mistake, add Oprah and success to the equation
Her heart is not up for debate

Relationships complicate things, appears easy to naked eye but that's because the discussion is falsely based on lucid imagery
Ms. Beautifully complicated,
I want to be your compliment, your crown so heavy, allow me to assist and adjust
It covers your eyes from the fact we both are royalty and there is no King nor Queen without the family
Ms. Back Excellence,
I'm only requesting a conversation in hopes to know you better
All talk no touch, the Sex is no rush
So, don't mind the sexual innuendos unlike previous cats I'm grown and I know it only flows wetter the better I get to know
Your beautiful, the image and shape appealed to me
Basic line, Ms. lady you fine and I get you already knew that
I'm flirting with the possibility of us but, first we need to establish trust
See that face you making, that line done fucked you up
I've past Mr hit and run; I only want to become your security blanket
Compliment you where needed, be a luxury to you
I got power couple visions too but, we gotta work from the ground up the, it ain't easy
I failed time and time again difference is I'm willing to try
Call me a hopeless romantic but, I got a love song I want to craft.
Ms. Beautifully complicated
I'm infatuated with you, however your layers of complexity confuses things.

Mr. Sidepiece

Hate the fact I'm such a great Sidepiece, I was never trying to be
But experience is the best teacher, played a game with Karma and she got me
Now I play by all the rules, never text, never call
Just wait and respond with your emojis of her choice
I play my role no feelings involved as you stated when we made this agreement
You'll contact me on your time only when you need those beneficial moments
A good fuck or an ear to listen to bounce your problems or ideas off
Basically, you'll call when he's fucking up his full-time job
So now the reliance is on me for that part time love
I bring out the beast in you, the freak you, probably teaching you some things that you go back and now he appreciates too
I listen first and don't speak, the shit that you want him to do
Support your ideas, simply see your views
Don't worry though I never will I tell you to leave your boo, I really don't want you
I'm a temporary fairytale, my job is easy
Secretly, I want to be in love and can't find my own piece
Not have feelings involved and if she creeps with me then can I trust the other side honestly
I look at myself in the mirror and I'm not happy with me
I'm wrong for my actions, lying like I'm helping her with he
That makes sense of it all
Signed Forever Sidepiece

Glow Up

Her glow up is special
Low key texts from her ex nigga
He's no longer relevant, left on red
No reply fuck him
She's prepping for sundress season and cheeky boy shorts are the indoor option
Oh she's #Summertime fine
This season about to be epic
She's motivated bout to make that fuck boy pay for his devious deeds
Guaranteed her next post on IG, he in her DM's with apologies
See you got the game fucked up, thought your dick was a shit
Oh, let me guess she told you that cause last I checked every nigga got one of them
Now I'm posting pics, trips overseas
#NEWBAE just to tease
I held back on options just to find out you were disloyal to me
I hope she was worth it
Oh, my bag she was a one-night session and you already served your purpose
Went to her with your stressing and found out it was nothing on the surface
It's your boyish essence that's what lost me
I was hoping you'd get it through the lessons previously taught when I said
I would leave and I hate to see you in your misery
I love you too much but, I'm tired of that feeling that I'm not enough
So, I'm leaving you alone, apologies are not enough and I'm not taking your calls
You can watch and like while I glow up maybe then, when you realized your lost your childish ass will grow up.

Without Women

Without women
There's no me, so I'm glad Adam chased Eve to that tree
Without women
We can't rebuild a nation because they carry and nurture the seeds so without her it's only a thought
Can you picture a world without women?
Men would have no drive, no mission
I mean think about it we don't dress to impress each other.
When the money earned is spent on the fancy cars, and the Rolex watch
All that flash is done for the opposite sex
When women around we compete different
Remember those ballgames in the park
Wink at her on the way down the court
Give dude that extra cross in hopes he'd fall
See in that moment we trying to eliminate who she's checking for
Oh! You was his girl, well not no more
Without women
Who would teach us love?
See daddy provides but, momma's the core, the soul of the family tree is usually the grandma in the role of matriarch
For that ma let me acknowledge your efforts
Remind you that your presence makes me better
A man is molded in the image of his mother and fine-tuned by the father figure
Bad news isn't all bad when she delivers, she helps me see the positively in it
Without Women
We wouldn't know what the grind is
See to this day she still fights for equal pay
Somehow found a balance out all the things she has on her plate

Woman, the walking definition of words like patience, discipline and dedicate
Since we don't say it enough Women we appreciate!!!
Without Women

RelationTrips....

I remember being in love over a cassette
Pick her up miss the track and got to rewind it back
We'd barely talk I let Luther, Quincy and Marvin do it for me
The mix "The introduction to a love story"
Remember being on the phone and just breathing
Playing no you hang up first, on three we both go together and neither of us get dial tone
What happened to that type of love?
Calling on the phone to talk....like is so in so home
Parents like boy what you doing calling my phone?
Here girl, you don't pay no bills so don't be on here all night long
Kind of crazy how early on we called it puppy love
Now transitioning into intimate positions, we all got a thing for dogs
What happened to love, trust, and loyalty
I was taught that those were the roots of love, the foundation of what grows above
Shit, we in and out so quick that the roots rotted out from limited fertilization
We ain't adding water to commitment, therefore can't grow from it
She brings a past, I bring a past, I remind her of him she's packing bags
We caught up in relationtrips…searching for the one and shit
Starving artist looking for one quick hit, no patience yet we lack the preparation
Attitude is single life is just safer
Only feeling the lust portion of trip, that other stuff we don't want to deal with
I get it some past woman 1960ish stayed because they couldn't leave those situationships
Those days are long gone

If she lack independencies then that's a deficiency or Maybe that's just me
I don't want control, I want compromise, Be the want not the need in your eyes
We can all learn from struggle love
Each one teach one be the example for

Don't love us

They keep killing us
No matter whether I got my hands up
Or yell I can't breathe
They don't hear me as if my English is not spoken clearly
They take a knee it kills me
I take a knee they blackball me
Claimed a so-called elite athlete disrespects country
I just want to be free
Exercise my 1st amendment right
Which guarantees freedoms such as religion, expression, and assembly
Live within in a country where I feel as though the constitution wasn't written for me
My melanin doesn't allow for certain liberties
Yet it's the land of the free and opportunity
Where the goal is to chase
Life, Liberty, and the pursuit of happiness
Yet we're faced with ideologies clearly meant to stop us
First example low income housing definition the projects
What happen to the 40 acres that my ancestors were promised
Built the land that feeds you and assisted in world dominance
Yet I raise my children to be socially awkward
Tell'em young King and Queen your skin color brings forth an image
Be careful, you're black there's no such thing as the victim
Yes, the lessons are true, you were at one-point royalties' descendant
And after 400 plus years still they seek oppression
Born free, though many want to see you back in slavery
So please you can't do what you see on TV, you must respect authority different
75 percent with a badge cool, 25 percent get away with racially motivated killings

Abuse of authority, the unwritten rule of the judicial system
It's not if they guilty, its what you can prove
And the body cam malfunctioned
Raised as middle-class black you can't afford the lawyer who's arm is outstretched
So those 25 percent in they feelings might just a kill another brother or sister
Even if you play by all rules
Damn shame first thing I don't reach for a gun but a phone to record you
Go viral then we riot
Now we not civilized people but, 3/5 jargon you snuck in your 13th amendment
Creating an unstable system for prosecuted victims
If blacks and browns fill prison
How is there no such thing as white privilege
It's become tradition
To hide behind a badge numbers
No charges are brought up
They chalk it up as community ignorance
Manslaughter, when it should be murder clearly
Why else would it take 50 rounds, Asphyxiation or 3 or 4 surrounding me to beat me down
I forgot I'm a superhuman cause my skin is brown
The fact that I survived slavery is amazing
I get it, the nerve of you people to learn adaptation
See years ago dependent upon address you wouldn't come to my rescue
Now we salute Americas red, white and blue the irony
Those same colors could cost you your life when they get behind you
They don't love me

Destroy and Rebuild

Way too much energy spent trying to impeach
Lets' focus that on ways to strategically defeat, so there's no repeat
In sports you're always taught away from home come prepared to beat both the team and referee
Let's learn from the current state of crisis
The enemy aligned himself with riders
All the while separating the masses until we look at the unapproved actions
It ain't all fun and games now, he televised the revolution
Used a nation's love for entertainment and led us astray with it
Twitter finger champion pound for pound
America is open to the hatred, sexism, lies and racist statements
Is this a change or what life was really like?
Is this still our land of the free and proud?
Where we have the right to manipulate the 1st amendment based off skin pigmentation while allowing the 2nd due to financial statements to kill the children and innocent faces as if we are asking for disarmament of a nation
We got too comfortable, caught with our pants down
Needed this wake-up call time to destroy and rebuild now
Amazing how hatred raises the popularity
Fear drives manipulation to say the right shit, family won't eat due to job insecurity
Ironically, this was reality TV
Filled with the perfect placement of enough distractions so that behind the scenes theirs no consequence for their actions
No matter whether we claim elephant, donkey or independence in politics
Michigan still needs water treatment, health care is of the greatest importance because the road to generational net worth is led by it, why is it that the school systems aren't balanced yet?

Women win but, get less?
"And when you're a star, they let you do it. You can do anything. Grab 'em by the pussy."
The irony in that Statement!!!
Open doors to #metoo movements, and upper-class racist Hatred towards our woman but, wait they historically thrive in opportunity
We shall see if one is crowned Nation's commander in chief
I get it the rich get richer while the poor stay in the box through regentrifications it's that old money law
Let's stop wasting the time is gone, got caught slipping once time to move on, let go of the Russian dialogue, they won 2020 elections vote in those qualified to do the job!!!!
Destroy and Rebuild

New ambitions

I woke up this morning and realized I needed a change
No more looking for in her, what I don't have in me
Realizing I'm part of the dating problem, I've been stressing the Queen
I long to be crowned king but, wonder is there royalty without family?
I'm using sex as a vice to cope with my own demons
Guess I took Marvin Gaye sexual healing lyrics and twisted the meaning
Between the anxiety, depression and the PTSD I'm desperately in need of therapy
But, I'm a black man and it'll make me look weak
So instead I seek temporary release in between her sheets rather than to talk out my problems
So its my choice to remain socially awkward not sure if I'm fucking her or she fucking me
So I walk around hand constantly in a clinched fist
Think pistol grip
On the outside I'm woke, internally sleep
My minds a little shop of horrors at times my thoughts scare me
I woke up this morning and realized that I needed to change
No more apologizing for my myelinated greatness
Our ancestors were snatched from their kingdoms and placed on slave ships
Thought of as 3/5 man and still worked to build a nation
Using that Willie Lynch dissertation
Either they separated the family by hatred or hangings
Crazy how words from 1712 still exist in todays conversations
They call it genterfication
Where that 6x9 iron cell is the new plantation
See, the prison system is a billion dolloar business and my skin complexion 12 is taught that I present menace

Translation I fit the description of "use that nigga to fill it"
I guess this is the government version of a go fund me to support black business
Even today separating families by leaving communities lacking the father figure
Now parenting alone is often on the plate of my sisters
For that mistake my strong black woman an apology to ya
We were born as a generation of dealers now our children are the users
Karma from our medicinal distribution which is confusing when there's a healthcare crisis
Where Dr's bypass the uninsured body to be left lifeless
Losing way too many potential young black visionaries due to prescription addictions
And we're way to busy seeking selfish reparations not to see the demise of education
I mean they not even teaching cursive writing to the generation so they not know what signature is
Why no class on the investment in stocks, bonds and trust funds
We still trapped paying ourselves over savings accounts
That make little interest
Why?
cause the full intention, is to not to build generational wealth
But continue the gap between the upper and middle class
I mean if I die today, why should my kids have to pay my debts
When the signing of the emanciapation proclamation was originally a move for better business
I woke up this morning and realiezed I needed to change
No more chasing love, I chased them away
I needed to find myself, patiently wait and let love find me

Mind state...

Let's discuss my Mental health
How my aniexty is ruining relationships
Cause everytime I see her, I see him
A Shadowy figure unidentified, yet my replacement
My Mind playing tricks on my heart, I'm
Having hallucinations of her cheating
Got me enduring several sleepless nights
Then the depression kicks in
Im having Vivid dreams of her with he
Sex faces and intimate screams got me
Questioning my reality and reviewing possible inadequacies
Wondering does he have a bigger dick than me
Do you call him daddy and simply lie to me
In an attempt to protect my feelings
These are my thoughts as I lay awake naked
When I should be trying to penetrate your temptation
I wonder
Do I not fulfill her fantasies, when will she be fed up and leave
Do I have hours, days, months or weeks
My mindstate is going against me
Maybe I should break up with her before she gets me
Then further scars my ego, and yes I am in love with you
Yet in alcohol is where I seek refuge, unable to Express my deepest sympathies
To you, not from a lack of trust but, I live in fear of losing us
I'm misunderstood, confused and the world won t release me it's a taboo
I must play by the rules, these psychological mind games
That torments the ego of a black man
As a slave I lost my love to the masters hand,

Never had a role model I could call dad to show me how to love and treat a woman
So my idea of a love is what's seen on television and I can't promise it shows like Love Jones
Therefore, I lack in ability to communicate my feelings
And you claim to not have time to raise a man
But, woman, I need you to help me be better
Soften my skin, carve me out of the same material
God dressed you in for you are of goddess decent
Use those super power cocommunications skills that you were born with to
Help me decipher the relevant and detox the bullshit
Help me get out of my own head as my heart doesn't understand
The rejection from my brain and egos scared and just wont .trust in love for very long
As I drop to my knees in prayer to let there be us
As it is said that God helps those that help themselves
I want to Stop this cycle of Anxiety and depression that's losing love
Replace it with loyalty and trust.

The System

There's a system inside the system.
We are design flaws, expected to fail.
Raised in the projects, a poverty-stricken experiment.
A Living hell this is to keep us in check. Key word keep
The ultimate scheme keep us in debt, no financial freedom.
Give you government support, you think free thoughts yet, you're still systematically in need.
See the cycle.
13th amendment written to imprison and remove civil liberties no citizen but revisited ways of slavery.
Look around at the comparison our blocks flooded with liquor stores and trap houses imported goods, we catch the charge but who owns the boat docks.
Strategically infest low income housing with a way to get out, distribute this dope as hope but, don't cross county lines we will come to you.
See they gave us free but, never land to feed on, a lack of education had us premeditated as robbers to get our eat on.
Slavery still exist if you watching just transformed…. into prison, just look at the numbers if not locked up brown skin turn to victims
Sound of the police no longer a safe haven if your skin is melinated
Our sentence for being called "niggers" is different charged as third time offenders with less than a half. This is to keep the house leaning in their direction cause you are now felon Your voice goes unheard they say you are a No voting nugga, we gave you that as a privilege. You fucked it up, but you had little to no choice.
School system got a test in third grade to determine your direction. As for the others we will simply make them feel like they are not part of the decision, and it's that failed execution; the reason we losing, That's the real trap house

Gave you a figure head, cause they heard you tired of working for the man, the next genius part of plan tarnish the legacy,
Notice how just before the switch of Presidential seat theirs an increase the brutality by police, make it his fault, they winning right now call it off.
Give them the entertainment that's what they seek and spark a twitter beef,
Your whole Presidential tour goal hate is to hate on your predecessor destroy all his credibility.
Don't worry them niggas be often distracted by likes and double taps.
#Fakenews, Instagram models and twitter beef
Gave them access for progress on purpose while also, increasing the diagnosis of ADD
So they attention span is weak; easily diverted we'll sneak
Selfish society claim they woke but refuse to lend their insight.
Keep them trapped in the system, use a revolving door technique let a few escape make believe Illuminati that's too deep
They'll stop seeking knowledge, take the fathers out the community
Preach sexual freedom, even legalize weed
Black lives matter, we like the theme
Trapped in a System within system
Give us, Us Free!!!

www.ingramcontent.com/pod-product-compliance
Lightning Source LLC
Chambersburg PA
CBHW031633160426
43196CB00006B/397